Naked Knees and Blakey'd Boots

Brian Lynch

A catalogue record of this book is available from the British Library

First Edition: May 2009

ISBN: 978-1-84375-336-0

To order additional copies of this book please visit:
http://www.prestige-press.com/brianlynch

Published by: Prestige Press
Pantiles Chambers, 85 High Street, Tunbridge Wells Kent TN1 1XP
Email: info@prestige-press.com
Web: http://www.prestige-press.com

Naked Knees and Blakey'd Boots

Reminiscences of a Dagenham Urchin

Brian Lynch

Prestige Press

INDEX

Acknowledgements xii
Prologue xiii
The Estate xvii

1 Life in the country 1
2 Dung Ho! 5
3 No spud in the fire 9
4 Naked knees and blakey'd boots 12
5 Fiddler on the hoof 15
6 The Globe 19
7 The Bushes 24
8 Scouting days 27
9 Of mice and beans 30
10 The Mild Bunch 33
11 Have they closed the tripe mines? 36
12 Somebody out there owes me a pony 39
13 Hitler tried to kill me 42
14 Swimming on a parquet floor 45
15 The Power in the pen 48
16 Well, thank you Robert Mitchum 51
17 Being prepared to bottle it 54
18 Hopping the wag 57
19 Heroes for a handful of marbles 60
20 Whacko! 63
21 Nothing but the tooth 66

22 'ancock, Robin and Cap'n Jim 69
23 A bootful of beer 74
24 The happiest days of my life? 78
25 Music was not my food of love 86
26 The chicken who crossed the road 92
27 No flies on Mrs Morrison 95
28 The Barking dog sang 98
29 We were all gropers then 101
30 Dudley Moore robbed me 104
31 Didn't we have a luverley day 107
32 Nice one Emma 110
33 Punchups in the playground 113
34 The devil galloped every night 116
35 Bring back those old time socialists 119
36 So where did I go wrong? 122
37 A little 'levver' shop in Romford 125
38 A nice quiet Sunday 128
39 Confession is good for the sold 130

INTERMISSION The sea-urchin 133

40 National Service 176
41 Nothing like home cooking 179
42 Don't they touch each other any more? 182
43 On the run 185
44 They told Dad the error of his ways 188
45 Well, it was Christmas, after all 191
46 Woolies was finger-nicking good 194
47 I saw 'itler at the butchers 197
48 No one kicked sand in our faces 200
49 The ragamuffin Olympics 203
50 Bell-bottomed Christmas 206
51 Pope Jim 209
52 Head over heels for Pet 213
53 We wore the luggage label 216

54 On yer bike 220
55 We buried the milk in the garden 223
56 The age of innocence,
    shoplifting and scrumping 226
57 The day peace broke out 229
58 Cream cakes and the latchkey kids 234
59 I wish I'd looked behind me 237
60 Definitely not Swan Lake 240
61 Forget Ferguson, we had Bert Myers 243
62 The potato poacher 246
63 Love in the glue factory 249
64 Anyone for Denis? 252
65 Hae ye gotta loight boy? 255
66 The Cameron I'd never vote for 258
67 Don't fly with me 261
68 Hearts of oak are our ships 264
69 A follower of fashion 267
70 Where's ya bin? 270
71 Blitzed 277
72 So, now I'm a vet 280
73 Jack Frost, the artist 283
74 Oxford, Essex and West 'am 285
75 Squelching down Rosslyn Road 289

Epilogue 293

Acknowledgements

For The Mild Bunch

With many thanks for sharing some great years

PROLOGUE

IN MY OWN LYNCHTIME

The war was over – we were safer now
The Luftwaffe could hurt us no more
It was time to live, to learn, and grow
To play, to laugh, to shout and to roar

They were the halcyon years of our youth
And we talk about them still
OK, now we're much longer in tooth
But we're not yet quite over the hill

We were boys, and they will always be boys
Playing football and cricket in the park
We made our own joyful levels of noise
Scoring winning runs and great goals, until dark

In our teens we discovered the dances
Got kicked out and barred from the Palais
We eyed the girls, and weighed up our chances
With perhaps Mary, Joanna or Sally

We queued for hours to watch Tarzan,
Mitchum, Cagney, Bogart – and the rest
In the Gaumont, ABC or the Odeon,
And on Saturday nights, went 'up West'.

Brian Lynch

We saw Max Miller at the East Ham Palace,
At the Palladium we laughed at Bob Hope
Days of fun and laughter, no malice
Young years to enjoy and not mope

We fantasised about Marilyn, Jane Russell and sin
How by their pools we'd huddle and lurk
So when they found us, they'd invite us back in;
But on Monday we went back to work

We drank frothy coffee in the Milk Bar
Quaffed Watneys and Ind Coope in the pubs
And yes, sometimes we did go too far,
But what the hell, we all had good jobs

Dagenham was a bleak sort of place in those days
In Barking and Ilford the traffic would clog,
Grimy streets, dingy shops - the memory stays
But they'd all disappear in the smog

Sometimes we really did have hot weather,
And since bus services then were the best
They were days families could picnic together,
In the quiet glades and peace of Epping Forest

Some of us went to cheer on West Ham United
In the days when Dick Walker was king
They seldom won, but we still got excited
'We're forever blowing bubbles', we'd sing

Nor will we forget those diabolical years
When some days we'd regret being born
Bullied by the insults, shouts and the jeers
Of Petty Officers all keen to perform

Naked Knees and Blakey'd Boots

They'd march us all day, doing rifle drills
Never a lot of time for slumber
Learning by heart, all the naval skills
And not forgetting that bloody service number

I did it my way, like Frank Sinatra once sang
Sailed the seas, and played many a field
Determined my life would go with a bang
And with real sense of purpose was filled

I'm so much older and creakier now of course
No longer in my absolute prime
But contented in my own mind, because
I did it all - and in my own Lynchtime

Brian Lynch

The Estate

The great 'Becontree estate', then the largest of its kind in Europe, came about thanks to visionary socialist planners in London's County Hall seeking to get slum-dwellers out of their East End ghettos. The arrival in Dagenham of the new Ford factory which needed a massive workforce close by, justified the project even more.

The architects the LCC (London County Council) employed built schools, parks, open and woodland spaces, shops, pubs and even churches, as well as houses of all kinds and sizes: but without intending to, they did so much more. They created whole new communities from which developed a real crucible of talent.

The estate gave birth to future entrepreneurs and top businessmen, show business stars like Dudley Moore, footballers who included Jimmy Greaves and Terry Venables and even great churchmen like the former Archbishop of Canterbury (Lord) George Carey. It also produced 'the Mild Bunch' – Buddy Blythe, Ginger Barratt and me (and 'my little bruvver' Roy), along with so many others like Eric Johnson and Billy Bowden.

Ford's arrival brought many other factories to service it making parts, components, even car bodies, to Dagenham as well as bringing in ships from its own Dagenham Dock. The ancient village was swallowed up completely by industry and that vast council estate which took up land not just in Dagenham, but in Ilford and Barking too.

Becontree Avenue, where the Mild Bunch lived, is a four

mile-long dual-carriageway - ahead of its time since traffic levels were nothing like as heavy as today - linking Dagenham, Barking and Ilford. Becontree itself was another part of the estate a mile or so away from the avenue.

The 'border' between 'Tory' Ilford and 'Socialist' Dagenham was a road called Bennett's Castle Lane and the house we moved into in the avenue was a hundred yards inside the Ilford part of that border. Telling the two areas apart was easy – on the Ilford side our streets were lit by electricity, in Dagenham by gas.

We lived through a war and then an austerity peace, raking the streets, playing soccer and cricket in the parks, shoplifting from Woollies and nicking apples from greengrocer's pavement stalls. As teenagers we Rock'n Rolled, poured into the Saturday Night Hops, the pubs and the cinemas in a way our parents could never have done. In their East End slums at that age they had neither the money nor the opportunities we had.

We never needed to carry knives, other than the penknives all small boys had in their pockets and, though often mischievous, we were bred to be basically honest. It was a different world – one where cell phones, computers, jet planes and even space travel was science fiction – but it was our world. It was one in which we survived, and thrived largely because we accepted that as a fact of life.

We were scruffy scallywags, street-raking rascals, urchins – whatever! It was history, family and our environment that gave us that freedom. Born just in time for Hitler to try to kill us, we grew up in days when you went into Woolworths either to carry out some petty larceny, or to shelter from the rain. Local bobbies whacked you with their rolled-up cycle capes if they caught you up to no good (or even for the fun of it), knowing no one would ever complain or report them.

Its odd but my most vivid memories come from those

days, before I was married. I have had a wonderful marriage of almost fifty years, with a marvellous woman, with whom I had some great kids. Yet, while I share some great family memories with them it is those 'ragged trousers with hanging underpants', 'naked knees and 'blakey'd boots', days that remain the strongest.

Life and misadventures with the 'Mild Bunch' – Buddy Blythe and Ginger Barratt, (the two Leslies) – and other lads who drifted in and out of my life, will be with me for ever.

While this book is not a chronological biography in the true sense, like those I have written for perhaps more successful men, it is a dip into my past through brief reflections and reminiscences. It is a past, that I shared with so many.

Half way through I have provided an 'Intermission' outlining some events that happened to me during the days I was a 'sea-urchin' in the Royal and Merchant navies. I may have been at sea in those years but at heart I was still a Dagenham urchin who never seemed to want to grow up.

I hope too that it is a peep back into a vanished world for all of those of us who came through those years – for, however old we are, we all love nostalgia. We can all relate to situations that our personal environments produced, even though we may have coped with them in different ways. From 1940 to 1962, through war and peace, this was my way, my life.

They are reminiscences of the urchin years I shared with some great people.

Brian Lynch, April 2009

1

Life in the country

When we moved to Becontree Avenue in 1940 I was almost five, so while memories at that age are often very hazy and confused some can also be very strong. Watching the Battle of Britain, Spitfires rising up from Hornchurch and parachutes floating down, not knowing whether to cheer or jeer, remain as vivid as those nights stumbling down to the shelter with the bombs falling and ack-ack guns blazing away into the night sky with the searchlights frantically seeking to light up a target. By the middle of the war we boys could identify almost every kind of aeroplane engine, British or German.

What I do remember clearly about our arrival at the house was the long grass in the front garden and the Anderson Shelter out in the back one. For mum and dad it was luxury to have even one garden, let alone two of them. He'd grown up in abject poverty with window boxes in Wapping, while she'd only known the tiny and scruffy backyard, with outside privvy, in East Ham.

That house, her widowed mother's home, was next door to the slum we fled from in 1940, a few weeks ahead of the Luftwaffe and I remember the hole in the passageway wall through which they could communicate. I used to be sent there to shout through it to 'Granny' that mum had the kettle on.

Now they were being exhorted to 'dig for victory', so

they were hunting down piles of horse manure left in the street by the United Dairies milkman's horse, planting seeds and cuttings, and building garden sheds out of old tea-chests made waterproof by layers of rubberised 'felt'. Dad even created chicken-runs and rabbit hutches out of whatever scrap wood came to hand, using skills he could never have learned in Stepney and Bethnal Green.

They discovered that some farms had survived the LCC's onslaught on their land and one of them, at the Dagenham end of the avenue, was a good source of bales of hay and straw for the rabbits and chickens that gave us the meat and eggs that relieved the pressure on the ration books. For our parents it really was a brave new world a long way from the shabby and dilapidated East End each of them had grown up in.

Their lives in the depression years of the twenties and early thirties had been of real poverty. Galvanised tin baths filled up in front of the fire to be used by everyone in the family, a single cold tap over a 'Butler' sink in the scullery and squares of old newspapers stuck on a nail in the outside lavatory. Now, with the trees and bushes we had along the central reservation of the dual-carriageway Avenue across the road to our new home, for them it was almost country cottage living.

The two up and two down 'Dockers Mansions' of East Ham had been replaced with a modern house with a 'best' room, with a huge Aga-type black-leaded fireplace at the front, a back room, a sizeable garden at the front with an even longer one at the back for them to grow their vegetables in (and around the air raid shelter), a larder and a scullery you really could swing a cat in (just).

Upstairs we had three bedrooms – well, two and a box room - and a real bathroom with its own toilet, although there was no sink to wash your hands in after going to the toilet or when you got up in the morning. For that an enamel bowl on a wooden box had to do but otherwise this was luxury in cold water.

In fact there was no running hot water anywhere in the house. For that in the scullery we had a kettle and gas stove, and a coal or wood burning cast-iron copper with a hand-pump to take hot water up to the bathroom. Although we took our tin bath with us when we moved from East Ham, it spent most of its time hanging on a hook in the back garden - apart from a few winter nights when we kids could bath in front of the fire downstairs.

My memories of that copper though are definitely not hazy. Every Monday (washday) it would be used for the family laundry, while on Friday's (air raids permitting) it would be used on bath night. Mum would be up early on Monday morning, having lit the fire to heat the water, sorting out the whites from the coloureds. Then once it was bubbling, full of soapflakes and 'Reckitts Blue', the copper-stick would be wielded to prod and poke the clothes about in the boiling water.

The scrubbing board (so beloved in later years by the early skiffle groups) would be brought into play to violently beat the life out of any dirt that remained. I suppose that was at least an advance on kneeling on a river bank beating the dirt out with stones. Then it was time for the mangle. Having wrung most of the water from the sodden and still steaming clothes by hand she would balance them as they went through the rollers while my job, if I wasn't at school that day, was to turn the big wheel.

Once the clothes were squeezed to dampness, and after filling the copper up with another load of dirty clothes, she would peg them out on the line. Washday would last all day so it did help her that for dinner that day we usually had what was left of the Sunday joint, cold with mashed potatoes and sweet pickle.

It was hard going and it's not surprising that we only

changed our underclothes twice a week in those days – well provided we had a change of underpants in the first place of course.

That copper – which a few years after the war was updated with a new gas-fired metal one - also provided our bath water and that meant hand pump duty. It was fixed to the wall and once you plunged the 'sucking pipe' into the boiling water you pumped like mad. The hot water would go upstairs and splash out into the bath, its speed dependent on how hard the mug downstairs (usually me) was pumping to shouted instructions from upstairs to 'pump faster'. That bathroom was also unique in one other aspect – it was the only room in the house lit by a gas mantle.

Years later, when I went to sea, I often had to pump engine room bilges with a hand pump and it always reminded me of bath night in Dagenham - and how I celebrated when they could afford our first bathroom 'Ascot' water heater.

But we had made our first move further out into Essex, from East End slums to a new socialist Nirvana further along the Thames. A short journey in itself, but a world of difference to us. It was here that I became a Dagenham street urchin.

2

Dung Ho!

We'd moved to the Avenue a few weeks before the Luftwaffe redistributed our slum in East Ham and at a time when our parents, who had never had a garden in their lives, were being exhorted on all sides to 'dig for victory'. For them this would have been a totally new experience and a long way from the East End they had both grown up in.

At best they'd been used to small backyards, barely large enough to contain the outside lavatory, a mangle and a washing line just about long enough for a few pairs of bloomers, long-johns and the odd shirt. All surrounded by a tatty fence to gossip over with next door. Suddenly they had what must have seemed like acres of real land, well scrubland broken only by the half submerged Anderson shelter at the far end, to grow their own vegetables, fruit and tomatoes. There was even room for rabbit hutches and a chicken run all knocked up out of tea-chests and wire-netting.

It was the tomatoes that really caught the eye though, even if it was only the sight of lines of them ripening in the sun behind a south facing brown-strip window, albeit criss-crossed with gummed brown paper strips. Yes, we had rows of potatoes, cabbages, carrots, runner beans and peas flourishing in the new gardens, back and front – even an apple and pear tree. Such crops were intended to help mum stretch our meagre rations and near-empty purses just that little bit further when it came to feeding the family.

For us kids there was even a patch of grass to kick a ball about (breaking the scullery window regularly), but for them it was instant farming with knowledge gleaned from newspaper columns and household 'encyclopaedias'. They were told when to plant seedlings, grow cuttings, how to sow seeds and they learned about the benefits of composts, fertilisers and how to create and source them. This was patriotic horticulture at its most intense – back garden farming helping to feed us.

Suddenly the milkman's horse became a useful provider of garden nutrients – particularly for the tomatoes - providing of course milkie didn't carry his own bucket. (When he did, we'd nick it from his milk cart while he was delivering down a long driveway).

Sometimes even during the war, we had the occasional totter (rag and bone man) coming down the Avenue, ringing his hand-bell to attract attention, with his horse and cart but his visits were very few and far between. The milkman, on the other hand, was very regular, even on Sundays and thus a potentially daily source of fertiliser especially useful for the tomato plants that everyone was growing.

Our part of the avenue was served by the United Dairies from its stables a few hundred yards away in Bennetts Castle Lane, but there were some unwritten rules about ownership of whatever their horse deposited on the road during its round. If it did so directly outside your house then, providing you wanted it of course, you had squatter's rights (so to speak). Outside anyone else's house and it was 'first come first served', if you could reach it before the people in that place claimed it. Generally speaking, our mothers kept a pretty careful eye on that horse as it progressed down the road bottles rattling in its crates.

Georgie Pickford, who lived next door but one, was my

first real childhood mate. We were about five, so were both old enough to be sent out on a dung-run. One day the nag did his dumping in the street just outside the house next door and, knowing old Mrs Donnison would have no interest, my mother hastily thrust a bucket and spade into my hands and sent me out to collect the goods.

I'd barely begun to shovel the still-steaming and smelly brown dollops of pure manure into my bucket, when I got a sudden whack on the back of the head. My 'pal' Georgie had also been sent out hotfoot by his mum with the same explicit instructions – 'get it or don't come back'. Sadly for him I had got there first so, in sheer frustration mixed with fear of his mum, he'd hit me with his spade.

I promptly did what any red-blooded dung-collector would have done. Our buckets were instantly forgotten, and the heap of tomato-nourishment ignored, as we rolled over and over on the pavement and into the gutter, kicking and punching the lights out of each other. A few passers-by curled their lips in contempt and walked on, leaving the two ragamuffins punching and wrestling with each other in the gutter.

Suddenly we felt ourselves being pulled apart by the scruff of our necks and held, dangling and wriggling in mid-air - Lusher had arrived on the scene. Our local copper - Police Constable Lusher, the bane of our childhood - lived a couple of doors away had clearly spotted the battle outside and come out to investigate.

Still squirming, spitting, wriggling, snarling and shouting at each other, Georgie and I were held at arm's length as Lusher waited patiently for us to calm down. When we finally did so, he read us the riot act. He told us in no uncertain terms that he was having no fighting on his patch, and that we'd better behave in the future 'or else'. Then, with a shove in different directions, he sent us both indoors clutching our empty buckets.

Mum, who had watched the whole episode from our front room window, was not very happy. In fact she even blamed me for not being quick enough to get the stuff into the bucket, before Georgie had even arrived on the scene. Then in the middle of her diatribe, she spotted Lusher riding away on his police boneshaker bike again, and shoving the bucket back into my hands, ordered me to get out there sharpish.

Obediently I dashed down to our gateway, this time keeping an eye out for George, but when I reached the road it was fertiliser-free. The only evidence of what had been once there was a dark damp stain on the road and a button that had come off my jacket during the fight. There wasn't even a sniff of horse-dropping in the air, it was so clean again.

But this time it wasn't Georgie – it was Lusher. He'd also spotted the equine overload as he'd come out of his house to go off on his beat, but by the time he'd gone back in for his bucket we'd beaten him to it and were fighting for possession. So to keep the peace he'd broken up the fight and sent us packing while he cleaned up the road himself.

Honest coppers?

3

No Spud in the fire

The old cliché that, 'its in the paper, so it must be true', carries about as much credibility as a party political broadcast, and as far as that is concerned I guess the scales fell from my own eyes very early on in life. It happened one morning when I was sitting in a very boring maths class in Rosslyn Road School in Barking. Our teacher happened to glance across at an equally bored classmate who was gazing idly of the window.

"Good view out there, is it Smith?" he sneered, hurling the inevitable piece of chalk in Smith's general direction.

"Yes sir!" The answer appeared a touch impertinent, and we all switched our attention towards what we expected, hoped even in order to relieve the boredom, would be a young ear getting whacked.

"Really? Well let us all in on the secret. What should we all be looking at then?" was teacher's sarcastic response, as he prepared to move into ear-whacking action. None of us expected the reply he got.

"Well, sir, actually the roof of the dining hall, because it's on fire". Within seconds desks and maths books were abandoned as we all dashed over to his side of the classroom. At that moment the fire alarm sounded outside in the corridor.

Yes, the dining hall was really ablaze. The roof of the big room we would shortly have been wrestling with rock peas, powdered potato and the gravy marinated gristle that passed for meat in our school dinners, had thick black smoke pouring out of it. Our classmate had actually been quietly watching it for a few minutes, but hadn't really felt obliged to let the rest of us in on it

Now we were hustled out, marched swiftly along the corridor and out into the playground to be counted and registered to ensure we were all there. The police cars and fire engines had bells in those days, not the sirens they have today, and the streets around Rosslyn Road were already echoing to their ringing as Barking's finest raced towards the thick pall of black smoke by now curling up into the sky. We had other people swiftly arriving on the scene as well.

Despite the pubs already being open, it was soon wall-to-wall local reporters outside. They were very keen to talk to anyone, but at first they were more interested in talking to our teachers rather than to us kids. Believe me that never took long to change – not with what we had to offer.

The fire totally wrecked the place. By the time the alarm had been raised it had taken a real hold. It had proved conclusively that the school dinners they dished up to us in those days could be ruined even more than when they were slopped and dropped onto our plates.

Now, the dining hall was on the upper floor of part of the school which had the dual-use biology and physics laboratory on the ground floor. Laboratories, kitchen tables, the lot – all were also well and truly gutted, that day. In fact we all got an unexpected and very welcome afternoon off because they had to send us home for the rest of the day.

The following day we made the national newspapers, because to earn a few extra shillings the local reporters had clearly passed on their stories and pictures to Fleet Street. The Daily Mirror, for example, ran the story and picture on the front, and continued it inside the paper. As an ex-journalist myself I have to admit it was a great story. They were particularly keen on the story of 'Spud' Murphy, our biology teacher and his 'heroics'.

A former Battle of Britain pilot (he claimed), dear old Spud wasn't a bad teacher, as it goes; though he did often prefer to talk about the latest episode of the Goon Show on the wireless, than the exotic lifestyle of the amoeba.

The Daily Mirror reporter went to great lengths to explain how Spud had dashed into the flames to rescue some mice that were kept in the lab. He had been forced back from the flames and had had to be restrained by firemen before having to give up his rescue attempt leaving the poor mice to suffer their fate. Great story – but it was a pack of lies.

As it happened when we resumed school the day after the fire, we had biology in an unscorched classroom, and Spud was clearly not a happy bunny. He pulled the Mirror from his brief case and angrily denied the whole thing

"I promise you all that this is total claptrap. All I did was tell a reporter that I had had some live mice in the lab, but I certainly did not give him this rubbish and I certainly never tried to rescue them", he said indignantly.

It was true – he hadn't told the Mirror any such thing. But I know a kid who had!

4

Naked Knees and Blakey'd Boots

The day would come when wartime and post-war austerity would come to an end and the lads would blossom. Drape jackets, garish coloured kipper ties (showing near naked ladies posing beneath palm trees) drainpipe trousers, from which would daringly peek a pair of daffodil yellow socks encased in shoes of all shades of brown with thick 'brothel-creeper' crepe soles.

A little later and the Teddy Boy with his velvet-collared jacket, tight trousers, string tie and winkle-picker shoes would emerge to pack the milk and coffee bars or prowl the Palais, beneath thick and greasy Tony Curtis haircuts and long sideburns.

That period usually lasted until we found ourselves being kitted out in khaki, air-force blue or, in my case, bell-bottomed navy blue trousers and skin-tight jersey. In fact, though they were not the height of fashion, for a couple of years that was the best bird-pulling gear around so actual fashion never really mattered for the boys during their national service.

It wasn't always that way of course but, like the girls with their first bra, we had our own growing-up milestones – like getting our first pair of long trousers, for example. Now that was style!

Those who remember Richmal Crompton's young scallywag 'William' will also remember his unkempt image. Scruffy jacket, socks around the ankle, a tie that looked as though it had served as a belt on occasions, hobnailed boots and short trousers. That was us in our scallywag days. Rain, shine, snow or whatever, we raked the streets in such urchin kit – naked knees, apart from an inch or so of grimy-grey flannelette underpants hanging below the trouser-leg.

We wore boots for very practical reasons – they lasted longer than shoes. Furthermore their life could be extended with the help of some metal 'blakeys', or studs, hammered into the soles and heels to save them wearing down too quickly. Often one of the blakeys would pierce the sole inside the boot and then the skin under your foot so that by the end of the day you were limping around like one of today's Premiership strikers seeking a penalty.

Dad used to repair our boots himself, using an offcut of leather he bought from a leather shop in Romford. With a deft slice of his sharp knife, accompanied by a stream of muttered curses as the hammer whacked his thumb instead of the nail, he would finish the job with a flourish of 'heel ball' – a kind of black (or brown) waterproofing wax.

Those metal studs, or blakeys, that he hammered into the soles and heels meant you could never creep up on anyone. In fact a bunch of kids running down the avenue sounded like a load of squaddies performing the opening chorus from Lullaby of Broadway, choreographed by a drunken NCO. Even on our own we could sound like Fred Astaire in clogs clattering along Hollywood Boulevard. But as far as real fashion was concerned for us boys, it was that much longed for first pair of long trousers that was the real milestone.

We never campaigned for them pleading the cold or wet weather or even our regularly scraped knees. No, what was important to us was not being the last boy in the class to get into them. We had mixed classes and it was hardly macho if you had the only naked knees in class not showing beneath a skirt.

Short trousers were cheaper than long ones of course but the real reason for our mum's reluctance to give in was because she liked to keep her little boys looking like little boys and not little men. So the annual trip to Woodmansees (in East Ham) for the new Sunday best gear (that enabled the current lot to become street raking kit) was always a campaign platform.

It took a long time. I think I was 12 before my parents finally decided that their eldest should acquire his first inside leg measurement, and I was able to pull on my first in a long line of clerical grey flannels. Wow! If I wasn't already secretly smoking Woodbines, that would have been the next step to manhood.

The next test of character came the following Monday when it was time to stroll casually into class trying not to draw attention to the transformation. Despite all the jeering it was nice to see the crestfallen looks on the faces of those lads still baring their knees and gritting their teeth in envy.

At last, real sophistication – elegance without the need to keep glancing down to see if your pants were hanging down, and with socks being able to fall around the ankles without someone shouting at you to pull them up. We had arrived, and now it was time to try for the yellow socks.

5

Fiddler on the hoof

We all know Dick Turpin was an Essex vagabond (an Epping butcher originally) with a predilection for lengthy cross-country horse rides after inviting people to hand him their cash and other valuables. He finished up treading air at the end of a gallows in York after a fairly hairy gallop with the coppers of his day hot on his trail.

But there was another, more recent 20th century Dick Turpin – and this one had a brother called Randolph who, like Dick, was fairly useful with his mitts. In fact he was so good that in 1951 Randolph Turpin shocked the boxing world by unexpectedly beating up an American boxing icon called Sugar Ray Robinson.

That same year the brothers Turpin also got chased out of Dagenham for holding people up for their cash, in a manner of speaking though not as blatantly as the original Dick Turpin had invited his victims to stand and deliver. We stood for it, but the Turpins never delivered.

It's all gone now but in those days the big eye-catcher at Becontree Heath was the Merry Fiddlers pub – a huge rambling institution with a sporting reputation that dominated the junction so much it even took over the name on the bus timetables. Behind the pub was a football pitch used by its teams playing in a local Sunday morning football league. In the fifties it was also the venue for regular wrestling programmes usually featuring the 'world heavyweight wrestling champion' Bert Assirati.

I have no idea how kosher Bert's claim to being the world champion was, but his name was always writ large on posters stuck to walls in and around Dagenham and the East End, long before 'Big Daddy' and 'Giant Haystack' threw their first paddy on TV in the sixties. So you can see that the old Merry Fiddlers pub had quite a sporting reputation in its day (I think it's a superstore now).

The ring they erected for the wrestling was also used for occasional boxing tournaments that featured many local fighters. It was there on such an evening that Randy Turpin came with his brother Dick, sometime after he won his world middleweight title in 1951. His success against the greatest American fighter of the day had made Randy into a national icon and he was touring the country in these 'play fights' cashing on it in a big way.

It was billed as an exhibition match between the Turpin brothers, and not unnaturally it attracted a huge crowd of local boxing fans. That included a bunch of teenagers – the Mild Bunch - who lived within walking distance in Becontree Avenue.

For Buddy, Ginger and me these were our 'tearaway' years before being torn from Mum's apron-strings to be taught how to kill, or in my case sink, Russians. We were regularly banned from the Ilford Palais, reshaped our toes by jamming them into winkle-picker shoes and 'flashed the ash' from chromium-plated cigarette cases with built in lighters. The lure of seeing the great Randy Turpin do his stuff in a local pub not far from where we lived was always going to be a goer.

So one evening that summer we joined the crowds at the Fiddlers and, glasses of brown ale in hand, we waited excitedly to see our first real live British world boxing champion. In those days such sporting heroes were always pretty thin on the ground, or more likely to be flat on their backs on it. Suddenly the murmur went around the crowd that a black Jaguar containing the world champ had pulled into the pub's car park. Gosh, it was really going to happen. We all dashed out back, with beer in hand, to get our first glimpse.

When Randolph and brother DickTurpin did finally emerge from the dressing room, the whole arena went berserk. After all, the guy really was a British hero (and lets not forget black, but even in those days it didn't matter) who against all the odds had duffed up a Yank boxing legend. The brothers climbed into the ring to be introduced – Dick was a top-flight boxer in his own right (they were both middleweights) as well – and we cheered them to the echo.

They got unrobed, squared up to each other and then went to work - well, work of sorts. Yes, admittedly it had been billed as an exhibition match, but it wasn't long before the crowd began to realise that we were being taken for a ride - and it wasn't on the back of a black horse moving swiftly in a northerly direction either. The Turpin brothers had no intention of standing to deliver, or of moving around the ring very energetically to do it either.

This was brotherly love taken too far, with Dick and Randolph just patting each other, laughing, clowning and seemly totally indifferent to the occasion and what it meant to local boxing fans. They were clearly oblivious to the fact that they were doing so in front of a crowd of Dagenham drunks, who were getting more and more unhappy and growingly abusive at what was going on.

Apart from what we'd spent on booze in the Fiddlers, everyone there had paid good money to watch some real exhibition boxing with good footwork and genuine world championship skills on display. No one was expecting blood and thunder violence of course but what we were getting was pantomime punching, comical clinching and Lullaby of Broadway dancing around the ring.

The previous Christmas the pantomime Old King Cole had been a sell-out at the London Palladium, but realisation began to seep through ale-befuddled minds that this was the night the 'Fiddlers Three' were appearing in Becontree Heath - all merry but only one of them being a pub. The two we were looking at weren't standing and they certainly weren't delivering - they were having a laugh, and we were the joke.

There wasn't an actual riot - well, we didn't in those days, did we? But cheers very quickly turned to some quite threatening jeers, and the brothers suddenly realised it was time to get up on their toes – and I do not mean in the boxing sense. They ducked out of the ring, presumably took their money and rode off into the night in their black Jaguar horse-power.

At least our home-grown Essex Dick Turpin had some class!

6

The Globe

You can't go through life without meeting someone about whom you can truthfully say it was 'hate at first sight', a person who you feel have marked you for life in some way or another. Yeah, I've had a few of them!

I guess Hitler was the first. From an early age we were mocking him by sticking a finger under our nose, holding an arm up in mock salute and goose-stepping all over the playground. We were all doing that long before Basil Fawlty, don't you worry. If the Wehrmacht had turned up in 1940 they would probably have taken objection to that little habit and shot a lot of kids, because they weren't renowned for a sense of humour.

Then, in school there were one or two, like the 'fearsome Frau', another German as it happens. Mrs Morrison who did her best to blitz some knowledge of her native language onto our tongues (when she wasn't battering them against the wall blackboard with her clumping right hook), was one who springs very easily to mind. Cameron, the one who 'rulered' me because he claimed (wrongly as it happened) I'd jumped the bus queue he was in.

But it wasn't until I'd actually left school and started my apprenticeship (at a wage of 35 shillings - £1.75 a week) at the Globe Pneumatic Engineering Co Ltd in Chadwell Heath that I met a man whose memory to this day I hate with a passion that even the odd touch of arthritis in my dotage I cannot curb. Yet, it is probably unfair because the guy was only doing his job and since as an engineering apprentice under his supervision, I was about as useful as a woollen hammer.

His name was George White and he was the senior foreman in the factory, so nobody liked him much anyway. A long gangling man he used to prowl through the factory just looking for someone to moan at – usually me. When I went back, briefly, to the Globe after my national service, his face fell so far he nearly fractured his chin on the floor.

My first actual supervisor at the Globe though was a guy called Fred Gilham. He was the 'charge hand' for the fitting and assembly shop where they put pneumatic hoists and drills together, before nearly destroying our eardrums testing them out. I guess, bearing in mind the job he opened my working career with, Fred was the man I should really have hated but he seemed to be a fairly friendly and reasonable sort of chap at first.

In the first hour of my working life he showed me around the factory which apart from pneumatic hoists and drills made other machinery like rams driven by compressed-air. There were two long and noisy workshops filled with benches, drills, lathes, grinding and milling machines – all of which meant nothing to me at the time, except that they all contributed to the general clatter and stench of oil.

After explaining that we were allowed a ten-minute tea break mid morning and mid afternoon, with an hour for lunch, Gilham took me to a small waist-high galvanised square metal tank about a foot deep. It was half full of what smelt like paraffin, and was, but beside it was a flat barrow piled high with cardboard boxes containing some metal bearings that even to my inexperienced eye were clearly of some considerable age.

They consisted of a split metal outer ring about two inches deep, inside of which was a complex set of rollers.

It seems the Globe had bought them as a job lot from the War Office because they were already fifty years out of date (and this was 1950 don't forget). They'd had a coating of Victorian preservative wax on them and my job was to clean all that muck off in the paraffin bath. The bearings that proved to be really rusty underneath the preservative I had to dump, but the better ones had to be greased and re-packed for use in the pneumatic hoists the Globe was making. (While I was there they actually made a pneumatic hoist to be used on Gregory Peck's Moby Dick film).

As long as I live I will never forget those bloody bearings and the stench of that bath of paraffin, as I stood there scrubbing away with a wire brush. Then, whenever I thought I'd finished one lot, Gilham appeared on the horizon with another barrow load from the stores (where, rumour had it, he had a thing going with the stores lady). After a few weeks scrubbing, a layer of black oily slime began to build up in the bottom of the tank, and with every new batch that layer got deeper, thicker and slimier by the day.

Half way the morning a whistle would blow, and we would all sit down near our machines and benches for a mug of tea. After rubbing some of the slimy paraffin off my hands with an oily rag I would join the other dozen or so apprentices to eat my sandwiches.

Around me, as I was scrubbing away in paraffin like a demented wick hoping no one would throw a lighted match in my direction, those other apprentices (and the Globe seemed to have realised what cheap labour we were) were taught the skills of painting engine cases, watching metal bars being sawn and seeing how lathe tools were sharpened. They never experienced the joys of 'skinny dipping' in sludge and the painful scraping of fingers with a wire brush.

Lunch breaks in summer meant we could go outside and

eat our oil-stained sandwiches, while during the winter we would huddle around the glowing iron coke stoves that were used to heat the factory. They were also useful in toasting the sandwiches on the end of handmade toasting forks.

One day I noticed that the skin on my hands was not only starting to peel off in great chunks, but was itching like crazy. At last I had a medical reason to complain to Gilham and perhaps escape the oily bath. Nowadays of course victims would go and talk to their solicitor, but this was the 1950s, not the 21st century.

I'd spent four months in that paraffin bath scrubbing away at those blasted bearings and now I could agitate for change on medical grounds. To be fair, he was very concerned and did indeed insist on a change. *'Tip that stuff out, scrub the tank clean and get some clean paraffin before you do any more bearings'*, he ordered.

I complained to White as well, only to be told to *'do as you're bloody well told.'*

There was one compensation however - by that time I had served my first three months as an apprentice and now my wages shot up to two quid a week. Then they decided to trust me on lathes and capstans etc.

To this day I will never fully understand how I allowed Dad to talk me into going into engineering. At school my metalwork had been on a par with my woodwork skills – dire – and the idea of working in a smelly and noisy factory had never really appealed. Anyway, I still longed for a newspaper office, but sadly had not achieved the right qualifications at school and that would take me another twenty-five years to achieve.

In retrospect though there were some positives, well one. Without the experience of the Globe Pneumatic (minus those bearings) I would not have had the alleged engineering skills to get into the Merchant Navy. That would have meant losing some of the best years of my life.

About three years after I started at the Globe as a cheap labour apprentice I went into the Royal Navy to do my National Service. When I was demobbed I went back to the Globe for about six weeks, because they had to take me on after NS - before making George White's day by telling him where he could put his job.

Because by then I had the necessary qualifications – and he'd given me the incentive – to sign up on the Southern Prince as a Junior Engineer Officer.

7

The Bushes

The 'Becontree' LCC estate was the result of a magnificent joint dream – by socialist politicians being keen to empty the East End slums, and Henry Ford being keen to fill his new assembly lines. While it is generally accepted as being in Dagenham, in actual fact it extended way beyond the old 'village' into Ilford and Barking with street after street of decent, if boring, houses which even had inside toilets and real gardens.

Those visionary architects also included trees in the streets – even little 'copses' on street corners - and we had the parks, Goodmayes, Valence, Parsloes, etc. All of which meant our generation grew up in a better environment than our parents had had in the East End, and in the Avenue we were even luckier because we had 'the bushes'.

Starting at the Robin Hood in Longbridge Road (a pub I see has now gone but was where Dearly Beloved proposed to me), Becontree Avenue still stretches right down for some miles to Becontree Heath; but now that first stretch is a dual carriageway with a wide strip of grass between the roads. In our day it wasn't grass – it was our Sherwood Forest, our Burmese jungle trail and the woods through which we tracked the Sioux, depending on what was on at the Saturday morning pictures that week. It also helped us often evade capture by Police Constable Lusher.

That entire stretch of road, down to the Ilford/Dagenham

border at Bennett's Castle Lane, was a long strip of woodland full of trees and bushes of all varieties. Each 'gang' of kids had their own hideout in the bushes opposite where they lived. Within a few feet of our front door we could climb trees, crawl through undergrowth to kill Japs and Comanche, or ambush innocent pedestrians with a selection of weapons that ranged from 'spud guns' that fired slugs of potato and catapults, to primitive bows and arrows. In fact it was catapults that that got us into trouble with Lusher...again.

Living in a house a few doors from ours he knew us and our parents – in fact he was the bane of our young lives. It was Lusher who once objected to our illuminating our guy as we begged in the gloom for pennies outside the newspaper shop in Green Lane, and made us blow out the candle on our barrow. This was the same 'honest cop' who once broke up the fight over the ownership of some United Dairies horse-dung between Georgie Pickford and me. He'd sent us home with empty buckets that day to face our irate mums, while he nicked it himself.

On this particular day he was just leaving his house to pedal off on his beat, when he spotted us hunting a big cat – well it looked big to us at the time – with a catapult. Problem was it was his cat and he'd caught us bang to rights and when Lusher hollered 'Oi!' you stopped and you listened.

Well, usually you did. This time we went up on our toes and scattered into the safety of 'the bushes' where we crawled under some of the deep thick bushes. Looking back on it, he obviously knew where we were – even worse he knew us and where we lived as well. So we were caught between two stools – did we give ourselves up and get bashed over the head with his rolled up cycle cape again? Or did we stay in hiding, hoping he'd go away? We opted for cowardice, keeping our fingers crossed he wouldn't bring it up with our parents later and in fairness he didn't.

After the war, with more traffic on the roads, the bushes were a clear road safety problem, so they cut them all down and made it a lawn. So, if a Lusher ever rides again, the local scallywags have nowhere to hide, but you know I always regret never having any photos of 'the bushes'.

8

Scouting days

A few years ago I kept a promise I'd made many times before, sitting cross-legged on the floor in Lymington Road school hall over sixty years ago – I went back to Gilwell, and ran into a bunch of school-kids from Dagenham on a visit.

In Scouting for Boys, Baden-Powell (BP) urged us to take cold baths if ever we harboured any 'libidinous thoughts'. To be honest, we wouldn't have known a libidinous thought from a dog biscuit – but our eyes gleamed at the thought of camping out under the stars and baking hedgehogs in clay in the embers of a campfire.

That was why I joined the 11th Dagenham – well that, and the glamour of the uniform. Bush hat (aka the Mounties), khaki shirt and shorts, and green neck-scarf held together with a leather 'woggle' (never did learn to make a 'Turks Head' woggle). In our eyes it was the stuff of the backwoodsman, though I have to admit that in those 'hand me downs' days, my first Scout shirt had seen service as cousin Joan's Brownie's dress before being converted on Mum's sewing machine.

I'd progressed into the Scouts after a year or so as a Wolf Cub with the 11th Dag, at a time of great early post-war national jingoism. Life then was a constant display of enthusiasm for special days like Empire Day and of course Armistice Day (Nov 11th), when we marched through the streets on church parades, sometimes behind a Boys Brigade band. Now it's just Remembrance Sunday which has taken some, though not all the significance out of it.

Youth was on the march in a way it doesn't seem to be today. Scouts carried sheath knives for effect, whittling and carving lumps of wood, and poshed up their leather sheaths with leather laces so they would look all Kit Carsonish on our belts.

Camping was the real attraction though – and Gilwell, BP's old home near Chingford, always the favoured venue. For ragamuffins whose only holiday was an occasional day trip to Southend, Gilwell was a dream. Even before our first camp we'd sat around many a mock camp fire in the school hall singing about *'going back to Gilwell, happy land'*, as well as that old traditional East End Zulu folk song, Ging Gang Gooley.

I swear Mum was a bit misty-eyed as she helped pack the rucksack we'd bought from the Army and Navy Stores in Green Lane, for her eldest's first time away from home. Old army blanket and groundsheet, along with change of clothes, knife, fork, spoon and 'two mugs – one for drinking out of' - were all rammed into the rucksack, taking care to ensure the blanket was where it would be comfortable on my back, and not a mug sticking into it.

We slept in old army bivouac tents, on which we would leave our hats overnight to flatten out and harden with the dew. Some Scout Troops slept in bell tents – all coloured brown of course because they were also ex army. Gilwell Park today is a palette of brilliantly coloured tents, but just after the war the shops making the real money were the army surplus ones like the Army and Navy, and Milletts. Like Henry Ford said about his cars having any colour you like providing it was black, with our tents and rucksacks it was khaki.

We really did learn woodcraft though and how to make

camp-fires with a few sticks. We didn't catch hedgehogs to wrap up in clay for the fire, but we did learn to cook bacon in ex-army (of course) mess-tins and brew smoky tea (from loose tealeaves) in billycans perched somewhat precariously over the flames. Our taste buds had new experiences then - wonderful moments that have never really been repeated, even in today's garden barbeques.

We built rope bridges between trees, learned survival techniques that might come in useful if ever we had to escape across Germany to the Swiss border, and we played football and cricket against Scouts from Newcastle and Manchester.

But I suppose the best moments of all came in the evening when hundreds of us left our little camps to make our way to the huge fire in the centre of Gilwell. There we disturbed the night owls and other nocturnal animals in and around the park, singing and lustily belting out ging,gang,gooley-ing in a variety of accents, without a libidinous thought between us.

Though there might have been a few funny Scoutmasters.

9

Of mice and beans

I read a letter in a local paper recently in which a lady complained about having suffered from mice in her house for months. It reminded me of my late father because when it came to catching mice, he could have taught that Pied Piper chappie a thing or three. He never used a flute, poison, or traps either - he used tins of beans.

We had plenty of household pests and the means to deal with them. We would eat our dinner with a sticky strip stuffed with fly corpses dangling above us, stank our clothes out with mothballs, and set nasty little traps for the mice. For a long time we also kept a tabby cat that, though he never knew of the undoubted pleasures of Cattomeat, did eat what we ate – or rather what we hadn't eaten.

For some reason Dad had a particular aversion to mice – he wouldn't even let them use our air raid shelter during the blitz. He'd actually been raised in the slums of Wapping where people had shared poverty with the mice, rats, lice and cockroaches. Out here in Dagenham - in 'the country'- we didn't have the lice, but we did have the cockroaches, earwigs and ants making quick skirmishes into the scullery (which is what we called the kitchen before we got posh) and we had the mice – oh boy, did we have the mice.

The oil-shop (they call them hardware stores nowadays) always did a roaring trade in mousetraps, flypapers and Harpic, along with packets of mysterious powders, crystals and bottles of liquid – all guaranteed to kill anything that flew, crawled or buzzed – even the kids. Watching the flies and bluebottles struggle on the sticky strips dangling from the ceiling above our heads while we were eating, was our normal cabaret.

Mice were dad's particular weakness, and for some reason he just couldn't stand them. In fact we'd left East Ham because he came home one night and, looking into the room where his two young sons were sleeping, spotted a mouse running across his eldest boy's (mine) face.

That made up his mind that we had to get out to some decent housing and we'd moved to Becontree Avenue as a result. Just as well really, because not long after we fled Telham Road the Luftwaffe reshaped it into a bombsite, so I guess in a way that errant mouse could well have saved all our lives.

We had a black cat to deal with them at first – but sadly he was so black he got caught in the front door during the blackout one night when his head was going through it just as Mum slammed it shut. Who said black cats had all the luck? But, Dad's favourite mice-killing weapon was a tin of beans. Now, after all these years, I can pass on his secret to any other mouse tormented soul.

First you take your can of beans and open one end. Pour the beans into a saucepan and heat them up while toasting a couple of slices of bread. Then eat the beans on toast, preferably with a nice cup of tea, for breakfast.

After breakfast take the empty tin and cut off the other end of the tin as well. The next step is to take the two ends and bend them to a rightangle. You now have two hinge-like shapes ready for action.

Find the hole in the skirting board where the little rodent has chewed its way into the room. Nail one side of the 'hinge' to the floor and the other into the skirting board to cover the hole. I defy any mouse to chew its way through a Heinz tin.

In fact there's one house in the Avenue that to this day, could still have 57 variety reminders all round its front room – and I bet it still doesn't get any mice.

10

The Mild Bunch

I suppose we all had them – childhood friends, mates, pals, 'our gang'. I had the 'two Leslies', and I don't mean the old music hall act of Leslie Sarony and Leslie King. Occasionally there were others – like Billy Blythe and Eric Johnson – but Leslie (Ginger) Barratt, and Leslie Blythe, known for more obscure reasons as 'Buddy', were the two other main scallywags of 'the Mild Bunch'.

Between watching the RAF having a pop at the Luftwaffe, swapping American comics and hunting for shrapnel, we played street soccer and park cricket and, after the war as teenagers, we boozed, bopped and got banned from the Ilford Palais.

As kids we lived life to the full – well, as full as it could get in times when everyone was skint, our food came out of ration books and the Germans were trying to kill us. We nicked cheap water pistols out of Woolworth's to run amok, in our short trousers with hanging underpants and half-mast socks, among the bombsites squirting anyone in range with puddle water.

Ginger once got me a real good hiding - after we'd dawdled our way to Stevens Road Infant School one morning. The gate was shut when we go there so we went home and were playing hopscotch in the street when my father arrived home for a mid-morning break from driving buses, and demanded an explanation.

Glibly I explained that the school was shut that day, but impetuously he grabbed me by the collar and marched me back to the school to check it out. Needless to say the headmistress was more than happy to mark me off her register, and then humiliate me as a corner decoration in front of the class till dinnertime. Then, when I got home, I got a whacking from Mum while Ginger, whose parents never knew, got away with it.

As teenagers during the fifties, we had a ball – well, at least until the government invited us to become soldiers (Ginger), airmen (Buddy) and sailors (yours truly). We'd started work, so we had money in our bins that we hadn't had to sponge from dads, or earn by getting up in the early hours to deliver papers and/or milk.

We went to Mr Doughty's dancing school in Heathway, so we could trawl for talent at the Saturday Night Hops in the Broad Street (Dagenham), and the Ilford, Baths, Seven Kings Library and the Palais. (Often dancing to the music of a local band led by a bloke called Kenny Ball – I often wonder whatever happened to him). At weekends we'd play football of course – in fact Buddy and I played a few games for Dagenham's 'A' side before our invitations to take part in the defence of the realm arrived. Halcyon days as we misspent our youth with great enthusiasm.

Buddy and I once went to a holiday camp – the one in Dovercourt that was later used in the Hi-Di-Hi sit-com. We spent seven days getting sloshed on Double Diamond, beaten at table tennis by little kids, and missing out on the talent because by the time we'd drunk enough Dutch courage to chat it up, it was all spoken for.

Looking back on our teenage days, they really were action packed. We laughed at Max Miller at the East Ham Palace and Bob Hope at the Palladium and rock 'n rolled to Presley and Bill Haley. We chain-smoked Woodbines out of shiny chromium cigarette cases as we cluttered up the

Black and White Milk Bar drinking frothy coffee at weekends. Then we'd queue sometimes three times a week outside the Regent (Odeon) in Green Lane, the 'Mayfair' (ABC) in Becontree Heath and the Gaumont in Chadwell Heath, to see Gary Cooper, Johnny Weissmuller and Kirk Douglas or lust over Marilyn Monroe.

Our finest moment? Probably letting down the tyres on PC Lusher's bike and then going up on our toes. He'd left it outside Ginger's house while he was inside alleging we'd broken his front room window with a hand-carved boomerang that hadn't worked. He couldn't prove a thing – but he was right because I'd made it at work.

Well, I was an engineering apprentice, not a carpenter – and anyway it made up for all the grief he'd given the Mild Bunch as kids.

11

Have they closed the tripe mines?

For obvious reasons during the war, as Uncle Albert Trotter used to say, food was a bit of a problem for most mothers. Our mum grew it, queued for it, or sent us to Chadwell Heath to nick carrots and cabbages from someone's allotment while they were at work.

In those days we chewed sawdust sausages, rubbery dried egg and downed platefuls of stew, with lumps of scrag-end (from the worst end of sheep's neck) floating defiantly among the dumplings and barley. God, how I hated mutton and I never developed the same taste for half a sheep's head my father had either.

Not everything was rationed of course. Offal may have only been available at the whim of the butcher, but you needed no points or coupons for it. That was probably why I developed a lifelong but now unrequited passion for tripe and onions.

Even after all these years my taste buds still tingle with frustrated excitement at the memory of those gristly tenderised pieces of cow-stomach, cooked in milk and onions to share a soup-plate with good honest boiled spuds.

After we wed, Dearly Beloved got my mother's tripe and onions recipe and, though she never actually tasted it herself, did a pretty good version of it for me. Then suddenly, for some reason it all stopped. Along with stewed eels and pig's trotters, tripe and onions became part of nostalgia.

I have to admit it would have been an acquired taste, initially based on that good old fashioned family 'take it or leave it' option. Throw in the added verbal blackmail about lots of starving children in Europe would have loved to be able to eat it, thrown in for good measure and there you have it. I mean, she was probably right but Ivy Lynch was quite unscrupulous when it came to persuading her kids to eat their greens, and she had some great emotional lines about tripe as well.

Knowing what our reaction would be if we knew the truth of its origins, she told us that it came out of the Welsh tripe mines, where brave men were risking their lives to get it. This of course kept us ignorant of the true source of our dinner, and even made us feel patriotic about eating it. In any case whatever was left finished up in the street 'pig bin' or fed to our own chickens.

This was the same woman who, when food convoys carrying only basic foods were being sunk in the Atlantic by the U-boats, unashamedly convinced us that the mashed swede flavoured with banana essence that she put on our bread for tea one day, was made from real bananas. I kid you not; when it came to conning her kids about their food that woman, bless her, could have lied for England.

Of course things have changed. We had a fishmonger in Valence Circus (next to the 'Continental Butcher' who sold horse meat) who would invite us to pick out one of the eels squirming around in a shallow metal tank on his marble slabs. We'd watch in awe as he decapitated the poor little sod, gutted it, chopped it up into chunks, and wrapped it up with some parsley in greaseproof paper for us to take home. Stewed eels is another of those dishes I can only savour in memory, though the jellied version is still there to remind us of what life was when Cook's eel and pie shop (with its green liquor), reigned alongside the chippie as our fast food outlet.

I suppose one positive is that they don't seem to sell a lot of mutton any more either, but where's the tripe? Presumably cows do still have stomachs – several I'm told - and we do still see them munching our meadows and producing that white stuff we put in our coffee. And, what about pigs? They do still have feet on the end of their legs, don't they?

It's been years since I stopped believing my mother's porky about the tripe mines, but it does appear to have vanished from our lives, other than in the tins we feed Jack, our Springer spaniel with, though in his case it's without onions.

Is there, perhaps, another EU regulation forbidding its sale? If that is the case, then perhaps a new sort of booze cruise, – a 'tripe trip' - across the Channel where they don't seem to take much notice of EU regulations anyway, might be in order.

After all, why should Jack get all the pleasure?

12

Somebody out there owes me a pony!

Back in the late fifties and early sixties you couldn't move in pub car parks for beaten up old vans with names like *'Ebenezer Scrooge and the Misers'*, the *'Dominoes'* or *'Harry and the Hound Dogs'* badly painted on their sides. From Liverpool and Newcastle to Catford and Cromer, bunches of scruffy young men with long hair were playing weekend gigs in ex-air raid shelters and pubs, before going back to the factory on Monday morning.

Dreaming of stardom the Scousers and the Cockney kids belted out rock'n roll and skiffle on second hand guitars, washing boards and old oil drums. This was also an era when being 'cockney' was fashionable along with whelks, jellied eels and spending in terms of 'monkeys' (£500) and 'ponys' (£25) was almost obligatory.

This new breed of alleged musicians was at least playing live music. A few years down the line and they'd be replaced by silver-tongued hippies with no talent above that of being able to rabbit at a rate of knots, but who owned a pile of gramophone records, their own microphone and a pair of very loud ear-splitting amplifiers.

About this time I came home after a few years in the Royal and Merchant navies, to start work in what I still (to irritate Dearly Beloved), call the 'glue factory'. It was a firm in Manor Park that made wallpaper paste, and it was where I found her – and have been stuck with her ever since.

(Sorry love, just joking – so there's no need for that rolling pin!) We spent a year or so courting in pubs all over Ilford, Dagenham and Barking, before finally fixing 'the day', following a proposal, which is a story in itself.

Weddings were not as expensive as they appear to be now of course but then neither were the wages. My seamstress sister Pat made our wedding and bridesmaids dresses; we booked a school hall in Ripple Road Barking for the reception, and found a cheap caterer to do the ham salad sit down for a few quid a head. Some uncles working in the docks provided the obligatory sherry for the toast.

We were getting married in St Margaret's in Barking which, because it was where Captain Cook did the biz, seemed very right to me as an ex-seaman. It proved to be a windy but dry day, Liz looked beautiful and everything went like clockwork – well everything except the music that is.

You see, about a year earlier, once Dearly Beloved and I had set the wheels in motion, my mother happened to mention that the son of a friend of hers was part of a band. This was good because although, as I have said, these bands were sprouting all over the country at the time, they were in great demand in the pubs especially on Saturday nights of course. So it was necessary to get one booked sharpish, and we did book Mum's mate's son's band.

Then, a few weeks before August 25th (which by the way happens to be Liberation Day in France as well as my non-liberation one) I decided to run a last minute check to make sure all was well. It was only then that we heard that the band, for which I had already paid a fiver deposit towards their £30 gig fee, had disbanded.

Clearly this was not good news but the lady whose son had been part of the original band, said he was still involved with a group and they would do the date themselves. Huge sighs of relief all round.

Came the day and we went through the rituals. We had our sherry, lunch and speeches and then had a break for a couple of hours until the evening. That was when we would be expecting the bulk of our guests for the evening booze-up and my father and I took the chance to set up the bar in a small anteroom next to the main hall.

We heard the guests arriving and the band turn up. Once the musicians had been paid the balance of the agreed fee in the shape of a pony (£25), they began to set up their kit in the main hall. Dad and I were just trying out the beer to make sure it was settled enough to be poured of course, when they started to strum up with the music and dancing.

It was just after that that we heard a few shouts and my brother Roy (the best man) came out into the 'bar' to suggest I came out because there was trouble brewing. I got out there to find that another band had arrived as well and the musicians were all squaring up to each other. Indeed the two drummers were threatening dire retribution upon each other with their drumsticks.

Clearly there had been something of a mix-up over bookings and eventually it turned out that the band that had just arrived really was ours. The first group had been booked for a wedding reception all right, but in a school hall further down Ripple Road. They went on their way and peace was restored – but I'd forgotten something until the other lot asked for their money.

So if a guitar-playing or drum bashing pensioner with a conscience, whose group was booked on to play in a wedding reception in Barking on August 25th 1962 but went to the wrong school first reads this, perhaps he would like to return my pony.

13

Hitler tried to kill me

Having written an article about my schoolboy pals in the 'Mild Bunch' – the two Leslies (Blythe and Barratt) - the power of the Dagenham Post was such that within days I was reunited with them – well, verbally by phone at first.

It was really great to talk to them for the first time in over half a century since the government broke us up with its insistence that we spent a couple of years learning how to kill Russians. Then I'd gone off to sea with the merchant navy and we never really got back in touch, even when I came ashore for good.

There will always be a special bond between us. We played football and cricket together, scrumped apples together, and we nearly got killed together, when only my father's cack-handedness saved our lives. So, now I have your attention switch off your mobile phones and settle down while I tell you how Dad foiled Hitler's last desperate pop at the Mild Bunch. I can even pinpoint the date - February 3rd, 1945, a matter of weeks before he blew his brains out.

We never had the kind of featherweight leather football they play with now. Ours was a heavy leather panelled job with a painful leather lace (if you headed it in the wrong place you were nearly concussed) and bone breaking soggy in the rain and mud. More relevantly it had an inflatable rubber 'bladder' inside.

In February 1945 the ball that 'Buddy', 'Ginger' and I usually played with happened to be mine, but sadly it needed pumping up. Dad offered to do it in time for us to take it over Goodmayes Park the following day, but there was always a problem when it came to pumping these balls up. When the bladder had been fully pumped up inside the ball, the rubber tube connected to it needed to be shoved back before it could all be laced up again ready to be kicked about.

On this night, once the puncture had been mended and the pump put to good use, Dad used the end of a tablespoon to press it all into place. 'Bang!' – The spoon slipped and went right through the rubber bladder. This time it was much too badly damaged to be repaired and even if we had the time and money (which we didn't), there was no time to get a new bladder.

The next day I had to break the news to the lads, and we decided to go over the park anyway and watch a match. This official game with adults, a ref and everything, was at the other end of the park to the one we usually played on - and would have been playing on, if we'd had a ball that day. We watched it and suddenly, midway through the first half, a plume of smoke suddenly arched across the horizon in front of us and plunged into the other side of the park. It was a V2 rocket and it made a helluva bang along with a massive hole, exactly where our coats would have been goalposts had we been playing that day.

Everyone hit the deck of course, because that is what we instinctively did in those days, but after a few minutes the game restarted and we carried on watching it until the ref blew his whistle. In retrospect this might seem a bit casual now, but we'd spent five years getting used to bangs and bombs, and we knew our priorities. Once the match was over we strolled over to the other side of the park to see the crater (which later became a boating lake).

There had been a casualty, but not in the park. A bloke in the barber's across the road had been 'trusting his hair to

Sydney's care' (according to Sydney's slogan on his wall) when the blast damaged his window – though not so much as he'd damaged the guys neck with the open razor he'd been shaving him with. The customer survived.

My mother was in Sainsburys in Green Lanes a few hundred yards away (in the days when that shop was all marble counters and queues) when she'd heard that a rocket had fallen on Goodmayes Park. She dropped everything and rushed home to tell Dad and send him up to the park to check on us.

This would have been over an hour after the rocket had fallen, and my lack of presence back home by that time filled them both with dread. Alarmed, the old man hot-footed it to the park to check it out, arriving only to find us strolling casually away from it after rubbernecking the crater.

They were so pleased to get me home in one piece, I got a bloody good hiding for not reporting in straight away. So Hitler did get a bit of a result in one way, but for the life of me I can never remember the score in that game we'd watched while he tried!

14

Swimming on a parquet floor

Life had got a bit dull - the Blitz was over and we were in that 'quiet' period before the doodlebugs and rockets got the sirens wailing on a regular basis again. So the announcement that school swimming lessons would begin, was quite exciting. Our first lessons would be held in the school itself, though there was one major drawback - Stevens Road never had a pool.

We would be required to have swimming costumes, and that caused a bit of a panic at home because I never had one. What I did have was a clutch of older cousins and eventually a family appeal produced an old costume - a woolen girl's one that had to be suitably re-designed by Mum.

Anyway it was with a great deal of anticipation that we turned up at school one day, complete with cozzies wrapped in towels under our arms for our first lesson, to be marched into the school's hall. That must have been a sight to behold - forty skinny boys and girls, lined up in ranks and most of us wearing make-do-and-mend costumes.

We were taken through the arms part of the breaststroke. We were shown how to put our hands together like we were saying prayers, shove them up to a point above our heads, and then bring them down apart in a wide sweep, back to the prayer position. No problem - within minutes we were all flailing around like a human wind-farm - or would have been, had they been invented.

Once we had the arm movements off to a fine art, we got to the legs bit, or should I say 'leg'. Like a flock of scrawny storks, we stood on one leg and did our frog impressions with the other, making sure we got the right co-ordination between our arms and leg. Every so often we had to change legs, but we started to get pretty good at one-legged dry swimming.

This went on for some weeks - we must have had the only swimming lessons where splinters and filthy feet rather than splashes and chlorine, were the result. Well topless girls their own age never do much for eight year old boys anyway. Finally came the great day. Clearly believing us to be strong enough 'dry swimmers', they crocodile-walked us down to the bus stop to catch the No.25 bus to Seven Kings baths.

This was the first time I had actually ever seen, let alone been in, a swimming pool. It took my breath away and suddenly doing the breaststroke Long John Silver style wasn't so easy. There was also another point our school-hall swimming teacher had forgotten to teach us - how and when to breathe. A couple of smarting eyes and spluttering mouthfuls of chlorinated water seemed to take all the shine of swimming.

Worse still I was not the only boy in the class finding his costume was falling down. So, apart from one-legged breast stroke, we were now trying to do it one-handed as well, holding well sodden cozzie up with the other. Well, we were still a mixed class, after all.

It was a couple of years before I could actually swim any real distance in water. On floors in halls, living rooms and lawns, I could swim like a fish, but it wasn't until I went to a school (the now defunct South East Tech) with its own pool, and a swimming teacher who could actually swim himself, that I learned to do it in water. To be honest I got quite good at it too.

I must admit it did come in handy during my National Service, because the navy rather liked to be sure we could survive in water for a while at least. Clad in boiler suit and plimsolls we had to jump into a pool, swim three lengths and tread water for three minutes, before swimming another couple of lengths. Those who failed were doomed to swimming lessons for the rest of their two years or until they had done it. For me the old parquet floor plunges finally paid off.

They did a few years later too, when I was a ship's engineer in a cargo ship called the Southern Prince anchored about half a mile off a New Zealand beach, waiting to enter a port.

Being officers we had some clout so, after a few beers and some drunken bravado bets, four of us were swimming ashore before you could say 'ahoy there, me hearties'.

OK, so we had a boat with us to bring the beer and sandwiches and to take us back to the ship again; but I still break out into a cold sweat when I read about people being taken by sharks in that part of the world.

We never had sharks in Stevens Road.

15

The power in the pen

I have never been one to shirk responsibility, and my life has brought me into many positions of power. I've been an editor and departmental head, navy officer (Merchant), Scout patrol leader, team captain and even shop steward, at various times during my three-score years and ten-plus. It's been a heady climb, which can be traced back to the moment I was handed my first badge of authority - as the ink monitor in Stevens Road Junior School.

Today we live in the wonderful world of the throwaway Bic, where hasty scribble is king and the well-formed hand that 'proper ink' encouraged is a rarity. Even Biro, the actual inventor of the ballpoint pen, is barely acknowledged as the man who put the skids under the ink monitor.

Yet it was a milestone. We'd left the infant school with its chalk, crayons and plasticine to move into proper desks with lids, long slots for pencils and pens, and neat round holes for china inkwells. They arrived gleaming and fresh from the caretaker's office, having been scrubbed clean by his wife during the summer holidays.

We were handed wooden penholders and gold coloured nibs, before being lectured on how to behave with the old blue/black. 'Your mothers will not appreciate having to clean ink from your handkerchiefs, or from shirts which have been hit from behind with pellets of paper soaked in ink. So you do not mess around with it...do I make myself clear?'

Having delivered her implied threat her eye fell upon me. 'Lynch, you will take yourself down to the caretaker's room and ask him for some ink. You will be ink monitor and it will be your responsibility to make sure all the inkwells are filled whenever they need to be'.

Wow! This was clearly the big time, and my rise to glory had begun - though I confess I was never trusted with the half sheets of blotting paper they also gave us every term. (Well it was wartime, after all). In fact, it was quite amazing that the government found enough metal left over from making shells, tanks and Spitfires to ensure the schools had sufficient pen-nibs.

Certainly we found them very useful, because a touch of heavy pressure on the tip snapped it, leaving two very sharp points. It didn't take long to find a way of attaching small paper flights to them, and we had darts able to inflict a fair amount of pain on an unsuspecting neck.

Nor did it take my classmates long to realise that the quickest way to empty an inkwell was not to dip a pen in it, but a lump of chalk. I tell you, some days I had more wells on the go than J R Ewing in Dallas. Of course no one uses them any more, and the days when the silence of an examination room would be broken by the rhythmic scratching of fifty pen nibs are long gone.

Then the fountain pens arrived. True they were in before the war and were very expensive, but you could fill their rubber storage sacs with ink simply by lifting a lever on its side. You could also empty it at speed, and distance, onto a collar in front the same way. The unlucky shirt wearer never knew about it until his mum whacked him when he got home. Lot more painless than a pointed dart, and much easier to disclaim responsibility for.

I held that job as ink monitor for my first term in Stevens

Road Junior and had clearly impressed because for the next term I was appointed as the class's milk monitor. My new duties were to go and collect the crate of free milk we kids drank in the morning. It wasn't too difficult to secret the odd bottle (they were thirds of a pint) in my overcoat pocket as it hung up on a hook in the cloakroom, to take home either.

It was an experience that served me well years later in the Royal Navy, when I had to take my turn as 'rum bo'sun' by going to collect the daily rum ration. That resulted in being given 'sippers' 'gulpers' by other recipients and being first in the 'rum rats' queue for whatever was left over at grog time and there always was.

Now that was power. Yo, Ho Ho!

16

Well, thank you Robert Mitchum

Once we'd progressed from watching silent movies sitting on a bench in St Thomas' church hall to the Saturday morning pictures at the Odeon in Green Lane, we all became movie buffs with our silver screen idols to worship.

We'd do our best to emulate Errol, copy Kirk, outdraw Hopalong and drawl like Humphrey, and hang around outside the Regent asking grown-ups to take us in. Because unless it was an all 'U' programme, open to kids, that's what it took to get inside. (Not to pay for us, we had the money but just take us in. You can just see that happening these days can't you?)

We all had our personal heroes - Gable, Bogart, Cooper, Cagney, Mitchum, ah there was one. Robert Mitchum was a particular 'God' as far as I was concerned. Mitchum, of the drooping eyelids and lip-dangling Lucky Strike, could whack 'em with the best. When big Bob chinned them, they stayed chinned and went down like a sack of soggy semolina.

I followed the man's career with awe, cutting out photographs from dad's Daily Herald when he did time for smoking pot, and committing to memory every word I saw him utter as I sat in the one-and-nines. That was so I could fantasise about the film and repeat his role as I went home.

Now, there was one particular picture, and for the life of me I have never been able to remember what it was, when he really did get to me. In it he casually stubbed out a fag in the palm of his hand, probably before he clouted someone. Of course what I didn't know at the time was that he probably had something in his hand to protect him from the obvious. To a ten-year-old goggle-eyed kid in the front row, oh boy was that impressive?

It was a memory I treasured for years afterwards - years in which I learned to smoke behind the bike sheds of the South East Tech, moved out of short trousers into long ones and began to experience all the thoughts and carnal desires of your average teenager. For a long time the vision of Bob's fag-stubbing routine was thrust to the back of my mind as other things like girls, girls and oh yeah, girls, got in the way until one fateful night.

I had been successful in persuading a young lady that I was good for an ice cream in the interval (while the organist was playing – do you remember them?) if she would go to the pictures with me one evening. We arranged to meet in the foyer of the Gaumont Cinema in Chadwell Heath, which happened to be showing a particularly tense weepie that week. They were always good for the kind of date I had in mind because of the tears they tended to provoke in the female.

I turned up in my best drape and creepers, and she looked pretty good that night too. It was our first date, after all and I guess we were both trying to impress each other with our worldliness. We went through the obligatory kiss and cuddle bit, she had her choc-ice and everything was looking fine - then she asked me for a fag.

Airily I whipped out my chromium-plated cigarette case and brand new Ronson gas lighter, to oblige. For a few minutes we puffed away at our Senior Service ciggies enjoying the film, with me getting more and more excited and optimistic about a result.

Then she leaned forward to stub the fag out in the

chewing gum that always clogged up the ash tray in those days, and that was the moment when the Mitchum memory came flooding back to me. Suddenly I knew just how to impress her with my toughness. Casually I stubbed my own fag out in the palm of my hand just as I'd seen my hero do all those years earlier.

Of course, it might well have been a particularly emotional scene but it ruined the moment for the audience. The sight and sound of a screaming teenager with sparks and glowing bits of tobacco (along with cigarette lighter which was still in my hand) flying out in all directions, was always going to be a bit of a distraction. It wasn't helped by the girl he was with screeching blue murder about hot ashes on her nylons, and the posse of torches that rushed in our direction down the aisle to throw us out.

The manager barred me from ever entering his cinema again, she did a runner never to be seen again and I had dirty great burn holes in my new trousers, but at least someone got a result that night. I never saw my brand new Ronson gas lighter again.

17

Being prepared to bottle it

I don't know if they still do it, but in my 11th Dagenham heyday the Boy Scouts had a fundraising week called ' Bob a Job' week where we would perform any chores for anyone, based on a shilling (a bob) minimum a time. The money was then collected and sent on to national headquarters to help keep the movement going. If they still do it, it's probably a 'Quid a Job' now – at least I hope so.

Now some people did take liberties. I remember a woman in the Avenue actually getting myself, and some members of the patrol I led and had brought in to help to dig her front garden over. It took a couple of days of really hard graft, and at the end of it she gave us…a shilling between us. Believe me it took a great deal of restraint, and obedience to the Scout Law, to stop us going back there one night and tipping a dustbin or three over her front garden.

In fairness most people gave us more than the required shilling – occasionally even extra on the side for ourselves. It was after the garden episode, which had left our donations forms looking a little sparse despite all our hard work that we did something Baden Powell would have de-woggled us for. He would certainly have taken my Patrol Leader's stripes away.

We were coming back down the avenue, disgusted but as true scouts bearing it in good grace, when we passed the off licence that stood in the parade of shops where Becontree Avenue and Valence Avenue meet. In my day it was called Clifford's Corner on account of the big drapery store that stood there then. As we reached the 'offie' a couple of kids walked into it with a couple of empty bottles in their hands, obviously taking them in to get the deposits back. It was one of those 'Be Prepared' moments when leadership initiative blossomed.

I beckoned my bunch of stalwarts and we went round the back of the shops where a small service road backed onto them on that side and where I'd remembered something. The off licence had a small yard out back, which was guarded by a very rickety fence and an even less stable ancient gate.

It was locked of course but peering through the gaps we could see that there were some bottle crates stacked up against that back fence, just where the gateway was. Yeah, you are right – within seconds we had hands pushing through the gaps in that fence and gateway sufficiently to liberate some of the bottles.

It wasn't as difficult as it sounds because to be honest the gate gaped at its bottom end by nearly a foot, so a 'scoutly' arm was well able to reach through. Then, armed with about a dozen bottles that we'd liberated from its yard, we went into the off licence to reclaim the money. We explained that we'd collected the bottles from our dads so we could use the deposit money for scout funds. No problem - the money was handed over without question.

In fact it was so easy that every Wednesday (Scout night) for weeks I went back to that gaping gate to see what bottles in nickable reach and reclaim the money on. It had to be Scout night of course, because no offie manager would ever question the morality and integrity of a Boy Scout in uniform. Not that it was going into scout funds after that first raid.

Brian Lynch

Nor were the 'redeemed deposits' gained from similar raids on vulnerable pubs, off licences and clubs like the Winding Way Social club just round the corner. In fact anywhere fences could be scaled or forced open for feverish fingers to grab empty Mann & Crossman Brown Ale and Mackeson Stout bottles in the months to come. It was usually safer than spending nicking time in Woolworths.

Ah, now that really was scam city.

18

Hopping the wag

I did something a few years back that I haven't done for years – I 'hopped the wag' from Stevens Road school. Since this was the second time I've done that I am hoping the result will not be as painful for me as it was last time. Then it was Ginger Barrett's fault and happened at a time we were ducking German raiders – this time it was down to a hot day and a German radiator

I'd pledged to go to my old junior school to talk to some of the kids about what a different place it is now, than what schools were like in my day. Actually I was quite looking forward to it, and I left Brentwood in good time on a hot and sunny day.

Almost seventy years ago I also left home in good time to get there. It was only about half a mile away up the Avenue and it was also already a warm and sunny day. Ginger lived a couple of doors away and we had our 'bushes' – the strip of land dividing the dual carriageway which was then full of shrubs, trees and bushes – to wander through as we went to school.

Well, by the time we actually reached the gates of Stevens Road – usually packed with a throng of grizzling kids and mums desperate to unload them onto the school– it was empty. Not a tearful child or anxious mother in sight - in fact there was no sign of any life at all. Ginger summed up the situation straight away.

'They must be closed for the day', he said joyfully and I was only too glad to agree. Obviously, we told ourselves, we'd missed the previous day's announcement that there would be no school, and there was nothing for it but to go home again – through the bushes of course.

There was no point in actually going into HQ (Home Quarters) to report once we'd reached our part of the Avenue. So, once Ginger and I had got bored bouncing off the bushes and crawling through the undergrowth, we marked out a hopscotch pitch on the paving stones outside his house and started playing there.

Now my father was a London busman (throughout the blitz as it happens) and often had to work what was called a spreadover shift, which meant a few hours in the morning followed by a few hours break and then a few more hours in the late afternoon or evening. During those periods between the shifts he'd come home for a spot of lunch, a quick kip or to dig over his vegetable patch.

This time when he popped home, it was to see his eldest playing hopscotch with his mate in the street, instead of slaving over a hot slab of plasticine in school. He was, to put it mildly, a bit curious.

'Why aren't you at school?' he demanded in a fairly threatening voice.

I explained that Ginger and I had turned up at the school to find it closed so we'd come home again, but he didn't seem to believe me. In fact he grabbed me by the scruff of the neck and propelled me rather rapidly back up the Avenue in the direction of Stevens Road.

When we got there I pointed to the still empty gates and said 'See?', but he never seemed to be taking notice. He dragged and frog-marched me up the driveway, past the piles of boiler coke stacked up near the boiler house and into the school itself. There, I was amazed to see, the classrooms seemed to be full and even worse the headmistress was not prepared to back up my story about the school being closed.

I was ushered into my classroom and there, in front of a chorus of sniggering and giggling classmates of both sexes, I was ordered to spend the rest of the morning in a corner reflecting over my misdemeanour. Dad went home and clearly told my mother all about it because when I did get home for lunch, I was given a b…. good hiding by her as well. Ginger got away with it because his parents never even knew.

The lesson sunk in because I never truanted again – well, not until that day recently. Then, on one of the hottest days of the century, my German motorcar decided that it might be a good idea to have a good old boil up on the A12 on the way to Stevens Road. By the time the RAC arrived to bail me out, it was too late to go to school anyway.

I didn't even have Ginger Barratt to blame this time, either.

19

Heroes for a handful of marbles

First we had the Dandy and the Beano, and thrilled to the antics of Korky the Cat, Desperate Dan (with his cow pies) and Denis the Menace. Every week we saw the misadventures of Laurel and Hardy in Film Fun, and Arthur Askey in Radio Fun. Well, it was a distraction from the air raid sirens.

Then one day we infants became pupils at the junior school in Stevens Road and began to put away our childish comics, for some more serious reading in the Hotspur, Wizard, Champion and Rover. Our role models now were no longer Julius Sneezer – the Roman Geezer – and Lord Snooty and his pals. No, now we had some new comic book heroes.

Yes, we had Dick Barton every weekday evening on the wireless, Roy Rogers and Hopalong Cassidy at the Saturday Morning Pictures, and very good they were too; but now they had serious competition in the paper shop. Our most regular heroes had names like Cannonball Kidd, Alf Tupper, Rockfist Rogan and the 'greatest athlete of all time', Wilson.

For most of us urchins, fame and stardom was a far and distant dream though for some of us local kids, like Dudley Moore, Jimmy Greaves and Terry Venables, it became a reality and was why we hated them when they did it. No, we lived our heroics through our serious comics – or the occasional American one that somehow contrived to arrive on the street's swapping market with well-thumbed Captain

Marvel and Superman in great colour. The Yanks taught us to read words like 'Wham, Pow and Shazam, written across whole squares of picture squares.

To us though the RAF's Rockfist Rogan was what Biggles had been in the first war, in terms of being a flying 'ace'; but he also had a pretty mean left hook when it came to the noble art too. Strictly a Marquess of Queensbury rules man of course, not a week went by when, after blasting the odd Stuka out of the sky, he pulled out his boxing gloves from behind his Spitfire seat and found some low life to beat up.

Alf Tupper – the 'Tough of the Track' - was another great favourite. There were no pretensions about working class Alf, who ran a one-man welding business under some railway arches. That was between pulling on some cheap spikes and ragged running vest to show a clean pair of heels to some rich and snobby public school runners.

Cannonball Kidd was a teenage centre forward who joined up with a famous old team after the war, in which they'd lost their own centre forward veteran. Week after week Cannonball would score the vital winning goal of course and year after year they won the cup and the league championship.

Another footballing hero was 'Baldy Hogan', whose team had a colour-blind goalkeeper - a problem they solved by having RAF roundels printed on the back and front of their shirts. Yes, I know - but they preceded Roy of the Rovers by years, and always played the decent chaps who never cheated, swore, played dirty or tried to get opponents red carded. Even in space we had our men – Dan Dare who appeared in the newly published Eagle was an instant hit.

We idolised our hearthrug heroes, and in all honesty tried to live the way they lived. They were our role models and fantasies and we passed them and their adventures around the street in barter and exchange deals, sometimes also involving marbles or cigarette cards. For us they were streets ahead of Superman and Captain Marvel – though to be fair we never turned our noses up at them either.

Anyway we had our British 'superman' – your average run-of-the-mill 200-year old hermit called Wilson who'd emerged from the Yorkshire moors and who, on a diet of roots and herbs could still out-run and out-jump anyone alive. With his high moral values and simple lifestyle, dear old Wilson was tops with us all.

Virtuous, celibate, abstemious and philosophical, it could be that he hadn't been in hibernation for two centuries – probably just seemed like two centuries.

20

Whacko!

Those of a particular age will remember comedian Jimmy Edwards' TV show 'Whacko', in which he was a headmaster whose sole method of handling miscreant boys was with the persuasive powers of 'the cane'. If he tried it now he'd have solicitors crawling all over him, and social workers trying to justify their existence by saying child violence was nothing to joke about.

Well, it never was - but that never stopped us being 'slippered', 'palm ruler'd' or getting the odd clump round the ears. We also needed to dodge flying blackboard rubbers and lumps of chalk, just for appearing to be daydreaming. I was once even put on trial in class by a physics master who accused me, falsely as it happens, of pushing past him onto a bus in the evening resulting in his being left at the bus stop. He got a result and I got whacked with his ruler.

We also had a sadistic German teacher, said to be a Jewish refugee from Hitler, who took great delight in beating up us boys, but more of her later.

I think the memory that sank in most of all was that of the school's head, Mr Claude Arthur, going into public whacking mode over some books. The South East Tech was divided into two – the main school in Longbridge Road (now a University) and the junior school in Rosslyn Road,

Barking, presided over by Mrs Coleman with Claude being the ultimate hot shot.

Once we'd got past the grief of school dinners most of us spent lunchtime kicking a ball around in the playground, or just hanging around in groups. We were doing that one day when some of the kids started offering us cheap Ian Allen train and bus spotters books. They were giveaway prices but I turned them down.

Not for reasons of honesty and integrity (being a Scout) you understand, so much as I was permanently skint, and couldn't afford even their rock bottom prices. It went on for a week or two before the authorities, in the shape of a couple of coppers, struck. It appears that the books were on offer because they were the result of a team of organised shoplifters from 2B who'd been nicking them from Wilson and Whitworths opposite Barking Station.

Caught bang to rights, they not only confessed but also even grassed up the kids who had bought their ill-gotten gains. Somehow the school calmed W and W down, presumably refunding the dosh and assuring them things would be sorted. Gawd - how they were sorted! I think it was the only time in my life when poverty actually paid off.

We were all questioned, with the buyers getting detentions and having to pay back the full cost whatever they'd paid. Then one afternoon the entire junior school was ordered to report to 'the hall' in Longbridge Road and, not being entirely sure why, we straggled the couple of miles to the main school. There we were all sat down along with the rest of the senior school as well, to wait.

The teachers - many of them in full kit with mortarboards and gowns - filed onto the platform. Then six of our schoolmates – instantly recognisable as the tealeaves who'd been flogging the books, also filed onto the platform. We began to experience the same feelings of awe the mobs waiting for the guillotine's blade to fall, would have felt.

Not excitement because this was very clearly a very serious occasion.

Finally Claude himself strode onto the stage to. He began to harangue us about some kids bringing disgrace upon our school by nicking things from local shops. He told us that each of the kids on stage was about to receive very public retribution. Then, as the others watched in mounting fear, he began with the nearest trembling backside to him.

That man pulled no punches that day. He wielded the cane he produced with such vicious venom we all winced at every thud – the recipients screeched out loud. It must have been even more agonising for those kids still waiting to be whacked as he made his way down the line towards them, especially for the last one. We had been urged from an early age to show that as boys we could stand pain, but believe me there was no stiff upper lip with those lads that day.

To be honest, I don't think any of us in that hall ever transgressed again either.

21

Nothing but the tooth

When I got together, after fifty years, with my old childhood pals Buddy Blythe and Leslie Barratt (the Mild Bunch) we discussed many happy memories - and deliberately ignored the bad ones. Well you do, don't you! I am really leading up to the school dentist who we equated to the same level as the Gestapo.

To be fair I haven't visited a dentist in donkey's years – mainly because since I parted company with the last of my molars, and changed them for nice 'washable under the tap' plastic ones, there is no need.

The fact is that when it comes down to the 'swill and spit' brigade the school dentist turned me into a devout coward, which only ended when I exchanged my last toothbrush for a tube of Steradent tablets.

We had regular visits to our school in Stevens Road, even before the Welfare State swung into action. (I am a great fan of Attlee and Bevan whose legacy of the National Health Service and social welfare stacks up a lot better for me than Blair's one of invading countries, 24-hour boozing and gambling casinos).

The 'nit nurse' would arrive to rummage through our barnets looking for livestock, and the optician would turn up with his kit – a postcard to stick over each eye and a white board with big black letters on it for us to read. By streets though, the dentist was the most feared because we knew that after he'd stuck his mirror in our mouth, prodded around and muttered some strange incantations to his female accomplice, Mum would soon be getting an invitation to pop us down to the Mayfield Road clinic.

There were only two forms of treatment – fillings and 'outs' - and only two means of making them bearable. They were gas and, would you believe, cocaine in its pre-Mafia days – but neither of them was offered to any fillings treatment. Touch of cold steel that, mate!

Terrified we usually had to be dragged into the surgery and frogmarched towards the dreaded black leather and chrome chair. Any remaining confidence, or at best bravado, was totally destroyed when they covered your front with a bloodproof bib. Then, with a merry call of 'Hold him down Nurse', they slapped a rubber mask across your face and turned the gas (which most of us had without being asked) on.

Suddenly you were out of it, dreaming about all sorts of weird things, before waking up with a mouthful of blood and a huge hole where a tooth had once been. We would then be helped out of the door, shouting and blubbering, by Mum and thus sowing even more fear into the poor little sods still waiting their turn.

No one who experienced those post-war school dentists will ever forget them and over the years I went to many of them very reluctantly before finally parting company with my homegrown molars.

In fairness it wasn't surprising that we had dodgy 'amsteads. Our toothpaste was usually a family block of Gibbs – a flavourless pink circle of hardened soapstone – and for some time after the war my brother and I even shared a toothbrush. Certainly it was a combination that gave me a lifetime of nasty moments even after the school dentist had had his way.

Years late a Royal Navy dentist, uptight because I hadn't

saluted him as an officer, decided to remind me again of what a cold-steel filling without benefits of anaesthetics felt like. He was also upset because I'd walked into his torture chamber demanding to know what more he wanted – an attitude brought on by fear of what he was, rather than who he was.

A few years after that and by then sporting a front tooth top dental plate, I copped a particularly nasty bout of seasickness when I was in the Merchant Navy. I happened to be running the engine room at the time so, in a bit of a rush made it to the back of the boilers, where the plate containing my two front teeth vanished down a bilge to be washed out into the Baltic.

Its probably part of a Danish beachfront now.

22

'ancock, Robin, and Cap'n Jim

A couple of years after my sea-going career was over I found myself in an historic Barking church pledging all my worldly goods to one Elizabeth Rose Denyer – at least that was the name she arrived at the church with. She walked out of there as Liz Lynch to start what has been over forty-six (so far) years of married strife… sorry, married life!

We'd met in a Manor Park glue factory – well at least where Wilme Collier used to make wallpaper paste – which had been foolish enough to offer me some employment as an assistant maintenance engineer. Our eyes met across a crowded conveyor belt and the rest is family history.

We courted in the pubs and cinemas of Ilford, Dagenham, Barking and Leicester Square, dined out in the new 'Chicken Inns' popping up all over the place, and canoodled in darkened shop doorways or at her front gate. Ah, yes seduction nowadays is not what it used to be.

All fairly predictable, but apart from her breaking with tradition to propose to me, I guess the final outcome was down to three men in particular – Anthony Aloysius 'ancock, Robin Hood and Captain James Cook.

Thinking about those three, one killed himself, another bled to death in a wood and the third got speared on a beach - flopped, topped and chopped. Now I have your interest draw up a beer barrel me hearties and I'll tell all.

Back in the late fifties/early sixties there was only one

television programme that could be described as compulsive viewing – Hancock's Half Hour. It went out, on black and white screens of course, at 8pm on Friday nights and was the first television show to empty the streets. In fact so many people stayed at home to watch Hancock instead of going out for a Friday evening pint or three, some pubs even began to install television sets over the bar.

The now long vanished Robin Hood in Longbridge Road was one and since Dearly Beloved then lived in Barking and me in Becontree Avenue, it was a very handy place to pop into for a quick Red Barrel (me) and Port and Lemon (her) at the right time to catch the show. We did that one night, found a table close to the bar in a packed pub with a good view of the telly, and settled down to watch Hancock and Sid James while quaffing a glass or two of ale (Babycham in her case that night).

As always it was a great show that night and it wasn't long before the entire pub was roaring loudly at the antics of our heroes. Suddenly I noticed DB saying something but it was during a burst of laughter so I couldn't hear her. I cupped my ear to show that and this time she shouted her question.

Now there always moments in television comedy shows when the laughter subsides, to give the performers a chance to crack new gags etc. It was at precisely such a moment that my companion raised her voice to go above the hubbub – except there suddenly wasn't noise, and the entire pub heard her.

'*Have you got any intention of marrying me?*' she blurted out at full volume, before realising Hancock had been forgotten in the pub and we were suddenly the centre of attention at tables and chairs all around us.

Now, you have to appreciate that in those days a question phrased like that had certain implications. They often involved irate parents or, in my case, another hurried look at my seaman's discharge book to see if going back to sea might be an option. Not that I had much time to think about such things, because I was choking and coughing on a mouthful of Watney's, spraying the stuff in all directions.

Right across the saloon bar of the Robin Hood heads were turned away from Hancock for a few embarrassing seconds, to home in on a crimson-faced young girl and her beer spluttering beau. Fortunately Hancock proved the greater draw and it wasn't long before we were left to ourselves again.

Once I'd recovered from the shock and style of her question, wiping my face and chin clear of Red Barrel I hurriedly reassured her that I had every intention of doing so. I told her that I had been waiting only for the right moment to bring the topic up. Oh yes and before you ask, she wasn't pregnant!

At that time she lived in Barking so her parish church, St Margaret's, was a natural choice anyway but then I discovered that a personal seafaring hero, Captain James Cook, had plighted his troth there a few centuries earlier. Well, what was good enough for Cap'n Jim was certainly good enough for former 4th Engineer Officer Lynch, so on August 25th (Liberation Day in France as it happens) 1962 we did the biz there too.

Now, nearly five decades, four kids and a granddaughter later, Hancocks gone, Cooks history and even the Robin Hood became a Longbridge Road building site, but Liz – I really did have every intention of proposing, honest! And just to prove it I am including a poem I wrote years later (see next page)

Liz and me

We met!
I was only just home from the sea,
She smiled - and factory gloom was lit
She laughed – her voice a joyous melody
In that moment I knew she was 'it'
That wide-eyed, dark-haired Essex beauty
Liz and me

We courted!
Our first date was to see Elvis,
One day we'd visit his home
But for then, it was just to cuddle and kiss
Hand in hand, to wander and roam
Dreaming dreams, wishing our wish
Liz and me

We wed!
In St Margaret's, Barking, on a blustery day,
There we made our lifetime vows,
Captain Cook had once trodden that way
Now we stood there, to make ours
Each pledging that neither would stray
Liz and me

We lived!
In a beaten up old caravan, lined
Up on a slaughterhouse base
With gypsies and travellers, but never mind
Yes it was a dump - a frightful place
But it had real people, the neighbourly kind
Liz and me

We bred!
Tracey, our 'Alka Selzer' Romford baby came first
Then, in Tiptree, Debbie turned up
David was next, upon us in Brentwood he burst
Family complete? No, one more for the cup
Emma - 'Oh God, three girls!' I cursed.
Liz and me

We laboured!
To give our kids their chance in life
We both worked many hours
Not just as parents, but as husband and wife
Through life's sunshine, squalls and its showers
Happiness, sadness and yes sometimes strife.
Liz and me

We made it!
Despite it all, we lived our dreams
And coped with the hardest test
Showed we were one of life's great teams
Our family raised and left the nest
Each knowing what 'family' means
Liz and me

And now!
We've got the T-shirt, done it all
We can look back with pride
We made our bed – set out our stall
And travelled far and wide
My God! We had a ball
Liz and me

23

A bootful of beer

It was Bob Davis who had the idea – or at least who picked up the mess deck buzz that led us to rolling out the barrel in a brewery.

It was sheer coincidence that we'd met in the first place. I was one of three National Service matelots being drafted out of Chatham to join the MTB (Motor Torpedo Boats) base (HMS Hornet) in Gosport. We had a leading stoker (months later we were all renamed Engineer Mechanics) in charge of us as we headed for Hampshire, and on the train he revealed that he also came from Dagenham. Even more coincidentally his father was a bus inspector and mine was a bus driver – both of them working out of Seven Kings garage at that time so knew each other.

Needless to say Bob and I became travelling companions (he lived in Bennetts Castle Lane – about a hundred yards from our house in Becontree Avenue) whenever we got weekend or long leaves.

Although Bob was nearing the end of his twelve years as a regular, like most sailors he was perpetually skint – a state even more parlous when it came to us National Heroes on 28bob (less than £1.50) a week. So as we were going home for a couple of weeks summer leave, he asked if I was interested in making a few bob by doing some casual work. I jumped at the idea of course.

I was even more enthusiastic when he said it would be

in a brewery – well, you would, wouldn't you? It turned out that he'd heard about a brewery in Whitechapel, which was always keen to offer casual (cash in hand) work to servicemen on leave. All we needed to do was be there by 8am and a day or so later, at seven o'clock in the morning Bob and I were on a 25 bus to Aldgate.

When we arrived, there was already a number of young, fit and clearly active young men with the dead giveaway cropped military haircuts waiting outside. Dead on time a bloke came out of the brewery with a handful of discs in his hand, shouting that he needed fifteen men. Bob and I got the discs that signalled we were 'in'. Surely this was a matelot's dream – we were going to work in a brewery.

Most of the lads were army squaddies with a sprinkling of RAF types but the common denominator was that we were all servicemen and, apart from Bob, doing our National Service. We were to be the 'chain gang' i.e. the 'muscle' that shifted full barrels of beer from one part of the brewery to the warehouse. There it would be picked up by the draymen to cart to pubs all over London.

Now some of those barrels were massive jobs that really did need some strength to roll them in straight lines (you try it sometime). In fact some of these barrels seemed to be under the impression that they were supermarket trolleys with minds of their own.

Our favourites were the little firkins, because they could be 'bowled' along 'Sir Francis Drake style' to each other as we waited in line. Dead easy job really – no brain needed, which was just as well since only Bob and I were navy (ahem).

All went well and then, about an hour or so after we'd started, an old bloke appeared among us clutching a half pint glass in one hand, and a clearly full watering can without a spray on the end of the spout in the other.

'Have you had your beer'? he asked, before filling the

glass with mild ale and handing it to each of us in turn. In fact he asked us several times and was always assured we hadn't, so he obliged us with more glassfuls all morning. Not, I grant you, the most hygienic way to take your beer – but it was free booze, after all, and by lunchtime we were all feeling pretty relaxed and happy.

We all went to the canteen for lunch and there all the full time workers, old boys close to retirement to a man, sat around playing cards and chatting. We, the young defenders of our country, were all flaked out on our backs on benches.

After lunch it was the same routine – pushing and shoving barrels, bowling the little ones along, but all of us with hangovers from the morning beer – a treat which was not repeated in the afternoon.

By five o'clock we were all shattered – bones creaking and muscles we never even knew we had, aching like mad and giving us real gip. However, we all perked up a bit when the overseer came back and thrust some paper money into our hands in exchange for our discs. I got more money for that day's work than a month of navy national service pay.

A couple of days later though, Bob Davis decided he'd had enough and would spend the rest of his leave in Dagenham, rather than the brewery. Being permanently skint I had very little choice of course so went to Whitechapel on my own. A few days into my second week though, tragedy struck.

During our firkin bowling sessions one of the army lads got a bit bored with the Francis Drake bit and decided that Ted Drake might be more appropriate – Ted of course being one of the great centre forwards of our parents day. It proved to be a great variation and we took to our new game, kicking the little barrels, with gusto – until one of us put his navy boot through the end of one of the firkins.

Even worse it was me and, as a couple of quarts of best Indian Pale Ale gushed out all over my boot, the overseer appeared again – and this time he wasn't best pleased. In fact he never saw the funny side and sacked the entire chain gang on the spot, leaving us in no doubt that our brewery careers were over.

It was great while it lasted though, and once our bones and muscles had got used to the exercise we were able to cope with it – and the free booze – quite well. No, I guess the biggest downside was going home to Dagenham on the 25 bus each evening. There, despite it being rush hour, other passengers seemed to set up an exclusion zone around us.

Well, to be fair we did smell like a brewery.

24

Happy days?

I suppose, from a safe distance of sixty or so years, Stevens Road was no worse than any other school of its day. Kids now seem to think they are being hard done by if they have to hand in their mobile phones and take their earrings off during lessons.

They don't know the half of it. For me, school days were definitely not the happiest days of my life, either before or after Stevens Road. It was one of the schools built for the new LCC overspill Becontree estate and consisted of infant, junior and senior schools. The estate itself was a massive development which covered parts of both 'posh' Tory-voting Ilford and 'definitely working class' Socialist Dagenham.

Though our part of the Avenue was in Ilford, we definitely came into the Dagenham class category. It was easy to tell the difference - in the Ilford part we had electric street lamps in our part of the Avenue, while across the border (Bennett's Castle Lane) Dagenham streets were still lit by gas.

We had moved into Becontree Avenue in 1940 - a matter of weeks before the Luftwaffe redistributed our old house in Telham Road to rubble. It was a stone's throw from West Ham's ground - but I think they were probably aiming at the docks rather than Upton Park. I was nearly five by then, so it was a case of 'new house new school', though of course it was my first one.

I remember when my own children started school they, and apparently all the other kids of their age, actually looked forward to it. We certainly didn't.

The gates of Stevens Road Infant School were jammed with screaming five-year olds that day, hanging on to their mums for dear life and grizzling as teachers almost dragged them into school so the mums could escape. It should be remembered though that this was at the height of the war when separations sometimes meant permanence and neither kids, or Mums to be honest, welcomed being apart even for a few hours.

The fact is that attitudes and teaching methods have changed quite dramatically. In our day school was more often seen as that dreadfully boring period between playtime and going home. Without exception my pals and I hated school from the start.

Of course it didn't help much when some pretty important plasticine modelling in the Infants, was being constantly interrupted by our Luftwaffe visitors popping over on their way to reshape London. At such times we were promptly marched into the air raid shelter - a brick built windowless building not even underground like our Anderson at home in the garden was – to sing silly childish songs.

Even in the junior school a few years or so later, many a crucial marbles, conkers or cigarette-card tournament was seriously jeopardised by some German pratt in France who had aimed one of his doodlebugs in our general direction.

As far as the V2 rockets were concerned - it never mattered because they were blowing people up before the air raid sirens even had a chance to start up and let you know they were on their way. The doodlebugs were very different though. You not only heard them coming from a long way off, you heard their unmistakeable engines stop and held your breath for ten seconds or so. You only breathed again when you heard the bang that signalled that someone else wouldn't be so relieved.

I suppose it would be easy to blame the war for the fact that we all had short personal fuses too. Few 'playtimes' went by without the words 'Fight! Fight!' sweeping around the playground. Immediately everyone stopped kicking balls about, hop scotching or, in the case of the girls skipping or doing handstands up against a wall with their dresses tucked into their knickers, to rush over to where the 'dispute' was already gathering an audience.

It was an established routine. Two scruffy short-trousered urchins, socks collapsed around ankles, circled each other muttering threats and invitations for the other one to dare to make the first move.

"Yeah?"

"Yeah!"

"Well come on then."

"Nah, you come on - why doncha try it?"

It got a bit boring after a while and reduced members at ringside to start shouting for one or the other to 'come on, do im'. Suddenly one would hurl himself into the arms of his enemy, to the roars and shrieks of the audience - particularly from the girls who always thrust themselves to the front to see better in the hope that blood might flow.

There they would cheer on the two scruffs on the ground, wrestling like mad, rolling over and over on the gravel - each trying to create damage on the other while keen to avoid it themselves. There was a lot of grunting and groaning - but very little actual blood involved to be honest.

The main tactic was to get on top and sit, legs astride the one beneath and gripping both his wrists. Now, at this point the kid on top would run out of ideas, because if he let go one wrist to thump his victim he stood a pretty good chance of getting whacked himself.

The one thing we never did was 'put the boot in'. We fought with our fists and arms - never with the boots, and I think it is a shame that in that sense we were perhaps more civilized than some of today's little rascals.

The battle itself would usually come to a finish with the arrival of duty playground teacher, usually a 'Miss' because most of the blokes were in the army. She'd been disturbed from the quiet cuppa she'd been enjoying in the staff room, so she was usually pretty miffed over the noise and chaos that had caused her to be called out.

It would end in a melee of teacher hands dragging the ragamuffins apart and marching them off to stand outside the headmistresses study. The cheated ringsiders would be lined up in their classes ready to be marched back in again. The 'action men' - neither of whom would blame the other for starting the ruckus of course - were usually 'slippered' or rapped over the knuckles with a ruler. All part of a days schooling, in Stevens Road Junior School.

We'd learned to live with all that, because it the way of things - but the most outstanding difference between then and now was the teaching itself. None of your electronic gadgetry, calculators or computers – no virtual reality tours of Agincourt or even mobile phones (honest).

What we had was down-to-earth brainwashing by numbers - spelling bees, mental arithmetic and mass recitations in classes that never dipped below the 55 mark in the register.

We recited everything from Sea Fever to the 'three times' table, either as a solo performance in front of the class at the behest of 'miss', or as a communal exercise by the massed tongues and tonsils of the whole class. We chanted on demand everything from the Lord's Prayer to 'Good

Morning Miss So-and-so', like a well-rehearsed chorus line or at the sting of a well-aimed piece of chalk.

Yet we would also be the lucky generation. We had the war and rationing yes, but after that we had the free milk, Virol and the Butler Act which decreed that all the nation's little rascals should have the blessing of a free education up to the age of 15. Then we had Bevan's NHS which looked after our physical well being, teeth and eyesight. Pity none of us appreciated it much at the time.

In fact we did have the advantages of some great technological and social advances our parents never had. They'd never had much in the way of paper and pencils – and dad in particular had learned his sums and spelling with chalk and slate boards. As far as other differences were concerned my father had certainly gone to his Catholic school in Wapping during the First World War many times without benefit of shoes or boots on his feet.

I had always been doubtful about that claim until one day I saw a photo in a book on East End poverty of his day, in which all the kids really were ragged and barefoot. We always had boots or shoes – with 'blakeys' or steel studs in them to help make the soles and heels last longer and made us sound like the third act of Lullaby of Broadway as we ran down the street.

I drifted through Stevens Road Junior, with the celebratory days off to celebrate VE and VJ days, with only a couple of playground punch-ups over disputed cigarette cards being the only things that really marked it out. Then I made one of my life's great blunders - I only went and passed 'the scholarship'.

Ostracized by the Mild Bunch

Once we neared the age of 11 we had to 'sit the scholarship', as the eleven-plus was called then. Success in this exam qualified you either to go on to a grammar, technical or other form of 'high school', though it was often simply called 'going to college'.

For me, failure would have meant the Stevens Road Senior School, which had all the promise of taking the first dead end job that came along when you reached working age, (unless you were lucky enough to get an apprenticeship somewhere). There was a lifeline for those who reached 13 and hadn't made it the first time though. They were classified as 'late developers' and given one last chance to impress the high schools with their promise and thus qualify to go to one of them for their final school years.

To be honest, at that stage I would have been quite happy as a van-boy - but no! I had to send Mum into deliriums of delight by doing what no one, even me, ever thought possible. I only went and passed the bloody scholarship first time at 11.

My reward was that I had first choice. That was the South East Essex County Technical School in Longbridge Road, though for the first couple of years we had to go to Rosslyn Road, Barking, which was the junior part of the school.

Even Dad got over-emotional – well, he did until he saw the list of requirements that came with the scholarship - uniforms, pens and pencils, and satchels full of sports gear. For me, though, the worst thing that happened was being ostracized by the 'Mild Bunch'

I had grown up with Ginger Barratt, and 'Buddy' Blythe, along with a couple of others, during the war. We'd fought each other for the milkman's horse manure for Mum's tomatoes, snowballed and joined in stone fights against the gang from the next street (Winding Way). Yes, we really had hurled stones and lumps of brick from a nearby bombsite, at other gangs at war when there was no snow about. We'd played street football with old and shiny tennis balls, and cricket using the street pig bins for a wicket. We'd hop scotched, marbled, and ambushed many a redskin in 'the bushes' that ran down the centre of the avenue - but suddenly I was bad news. I was a 'college kid' and, in their eyes, a snob, and it was a long time before I became acceptable again.

Even worse I had to go from the standard scruffy urchin kit of ragged pullover, stained jacket, and short trousers with hanging underpants – to blue blazer, grey flannel long trousers, white shirt and school tie, not forgetting that bloody school-cap. Even the shoes had to get used to a very regular, albeit unaccustomed, dab or two of Cherry Blossom followed by a vigorous brushing.

It all proved to be a bit of a false dawn as far as I was concerned. Within a few weeks of reaching the 'tech' I was clod of the month so often they could have built a golf course with my school reports. My only excuse being that because of the accident of my date of birth coming after the start of the school year, I was about six months younger than any of my classmates.

In fact, half way through my two years at Rosslyn Road, I was put back a year so suddenly I was half a year older than my new classmates. Didn't make a blind bit of difference! Mum and Dad were mystified. How could their oldest child, smart enough to win the scholarship at his first attempt, then turn out to be about as useful as a luminous sundial?

Algebra? Geometry? Logarithms? I had trouble even spelling them, and as for languages, well, it was a good job the war was over before I could become an RAF fighter pilot ace. The amount of German Mrs (Frau) Morrison - a Jewish lady of German extraction who had fled to this country before the war - managed to cram into me wouldn't have got me into Stalag Luft 3, let alone out of it. Mind you, Mrs M did have other unforgettable tendencies.

Apart from a thick guttural accent, she was built like the

proverbial barn door with hands like shovels and she had a very neat line in blackboard ear-thumping. Upset her, and she would carefully position you alongside the wall blackboard before giving you a pretty hefty clout around the ear that sent your head bouncing off the board. Since this was only a few years after the war, you can imagine what we called this lady and how much we speculated on who'd trained her, and where.

English wasn't much better either - in fact the only reason I developed a passing command of it was down more to the Hotspur and Wizard comics, than to the sad post-war parade of recently demobbed and frustrated novelists they employed to teach us.

Still, you know what they say about English. If at first you don't succeed...quit, and become a journalist.

25

Music was not my food of love

One of the great sadness's I have in life is that although I grew up in a house which had its own piano - regularly dusted and polished - in the 'best' or front room, I never got much further on it than a hesitant one-fingered version of God Save the King (as we had then).

I suppose my other claim to musical fame is that I was a member of the Valence House library at the same time as Dudley Moore who lived near me and we walked home together a couple of times. As far as musical appreciation in general was concerned, that was slightly inhibited by some German 'clout', and Fat Mary of 2C who came between Mozart and me.

Our piano spent its days largely as a family ornament - a highly polished dust-trap whose top served as a shelf, upon which rested framed photos of Mum and Dad's wedding and a coloured glass bowl which only ever saw active service at Christmas when it held nuts.

The keyboard part of the piano only saw action on those rare occasions when we had something to celebrate and had parties. Mum came into her own then, because she was the only one in the family who could get any kind of recognisable tune out of it. She couldn't read a note of music, but she could belt out a tune on the ivories.

So at Christmas, VE and VJ-days and the odd birthday bash, she would be pressed into sitting down at the

'Joanna', and soon had all the aunts and uncles singing about Mother Macrae, taking Kathleen home again, or that real party pooper 'We'll meet again' - which left everyone so emotional they couldn't sing any more anyway.

I can see Dad to this day, half-empty glass of brown ale in hand, leaning on the top of the piano, with tears almost pouring down his face as he slurred the words about that dear old land 'across the Irish Sea'. That was a bit strong for a Wapping cockney lad whose only experience of crossing water had been on the Woolwich free ferry or on a tram over Tower Bridge, though to be fair he did have Irish ancestors.

There were some memorable musical moments though. Not long after VE day for instance, we had a street party where all us kids had fish-paste sandwiches followed by red jelly and pink blanc mange, washed down with lemon barley water. Meanwhile the adults poured copious amounts of brown ale and shandies down their throats as they sang like the bunch of drunks they deserved to be that day.

Our piano was manhandled out of the best room into the street and Mum was thumping away at all the old patriotic throat-catchers like 'There'll always be an England' along with the highly cultural renditions of 'Knees up Mother Brown'. The whole street partied that day and burned anything that the Luftwaffe hadn't already burnt, on a massive bonfire in the middle of the road.

Sadly, Mum never passed on her musical talent to me, though I did make a tentative start, at the age of six. I was the 'lead triangle' in the Stevens Road Infants Percussion Band, but that was about it. There were odd moments of musical culture to come, like a few years later at the 'Tech', when I helped form the 3C3 'paper and comb' washroom combo.

That broke up after we got a detention because we had

been so absorbed in our own interpretation of 'She'll Be Coming Round the Mountain When She Comes', that we'd totally forgotten about the biology lesson we should have been involved in.

There were some opportunities to acquire some appreciation of music at the Tech though. While doing our first couple of years in the Rosslyn Road (Barking) part of the school, apart from music lessons, we had the regular concerts by the legendary Barking Quintet.

Our music teacher, Miss Shepherd, was a meek little soul who was totally out of her depth in the teaching business and we played her unmercifully. Her only means of keeping control of our kind of uncultured scruffs was to despatch the unruly to report to her friend, Mrs Morrison, the German teacher. Mrs M was a huge German-born lady whose guttural English made her sound even more formidable to us, bearing in mind this was barely a couple of years after the war.

Rumour had it that she had been one of the Jewish refugees who had fled from Hitler's unfriendly society during the thirties, had married over here but had lost her husband during the war. Now she was teaching us her native language and, as far as we were concerned, she was not nice people - possibly because half of us couldn't understand most what she was saying most of the time.

As I said, this was not long after the end of the war and we kids all had some less than fond memories of Germans and that wasn't helped by some of the revelations that were still coming out at the time. Because the 'fearsome Frau' was German and in our eyes a bully, you can imagine where we speculated that she had been trained, and by whom. Believe me this lady did not take prisoners.

So Miss Shepherd knew exactly what she was doing when she sent us over to her friend. We, the naughty ones playing up, would soon be trooping one by one across the quadrangle to Mrs Morrison's class, timidly entering to a chorus of giggling from a class relieved at yet another interruption to their German lesson. They knew, and we knew, we were about to be beaten up for their entertainment.

The old cow would look up and glare as we opened the classroom door and nervously approached. She would gesture us to stand to the side of her, sideways on to the wall-blackboard. Very often there was already a line of our own classmates facing the wall.

"Vat are you here for?" She already knew why and we hardly got the words out that Miss Shepherd had sent us over, before she spat out 'Vy?' We would start to stammer we had been messing about a bit, but even as we did her beefy right hand was sweeping up with unerring accuracy to clump us on the side of the face.

The blow sent the head jerking right onto the blackboard she had positioned her victim against, bouncing off just in time to catch the next right-hander on its way up. Then, still seeing stars and listening to bells ringing in our ears, we were gestured to join the line-up and wait for the next victim to be evicted by Miss S.

Still, despite the pain and shock, even that was a bit of a relief from the crochets and semi-quavers Miss Shepherd was failing so badly to inspire any kind of enthusiasm about 'proper' music into us. But, we also had the Barking Quintet.

This was a strolling band of musical worthies who had a contract with schools in Barking. They had the near impossible task of shoving some sort of musical and cultural appreciation of 'posh' music, into what were effectively street-rakers straight off the bombsite playgrounds.

Most of us found them about as welcome as toothache, but these were command performances - by command of

Miss Coleman, the headmistress. She was determined that we would enjoy the delights of Mozart and learn to appreciate the finer points of the violin, viola, and bass etc. To be honest - no chance!

On Quintet days, each class was marched in an orderly fashion across the quadrangle, and into the dinner hall cum assembly hall. There we would sit cross-legged on the splintery parquet floor staring miserably at the empty chairs, music stands, violin cases and big bass fiddle, at the front. We would be shushed as the members of the group filed in, presumably having been liberally entertained in Miss Coleman's office beforehand. As they made themselves comfortable and ready for their recital, our teachers legged it and left us to it.

By the time the lead violinist had started his chat about Mozart, Brahms or whoever, most of the staff were living it up well out of earshot in the staff-room. Only a few eagle eyed music appreciators like Miss Shepherd of course, were left to pick up on any of us not paying attention.

The up-side was that, provided you were sitting at the back of the hall or was hunched up behind someone like 'Fat Mary' of 2C2 you could read the Hotspur in peace, with little fear of having it confiscated and copping a detention. Certainly no trips across the quad to the Fearsome Frau were on offer.

Nowadays I enjoy music very much and of all kinds - even the 'posh' stuff. Being raised on Anne Ziegler and Webster Booth, the Andrew Sisters, Vera Lynn and Bud Flanagan however, was no real preparation for Sibelius, Shostakovich or Grieg. A few years further on and dance music - ballroom or jazz - would be a very necessary part of our lives for the bird-pulling Saturday nights at the Ilford Palais and Broad Street baths. At the time of the Quintet though, we post-war scruffs had all the musical appreciation of a forklift truck.

We may have been the generation that, a few years later, launched Rock n Roll, but the Barking Quintet never had us bopping in the aisles the way Bill Haley and Buddy Holly did. No one - as far as I know - has ever rioted or ripped up the seats in Covent Garden's Royal Opera House after getting carried away by the likes of Verdi or the voice of Pavarotti.

Mind you some small nods of music appreciation were beginning to penetrate our skulls. Jazz, Jolson and Glenn Miller were already becoming heroes to some of us, even before Hollywood started to rewrite their life stories. Then, in our teenage years your Frankie Laines and Guy Mitchells would be going on about Ghost Riders and Red Feathers on gramophones that usually reached us via some pretty dubious routes BE (Before Elvis).

But as far as our musical education went, your Bach and Beethoven, Brahms (and not forgetting Liszt of course), were probably set back years as a result of having culture thrust upon us by the well-meaning and very real skills of 'the quintet', who were decidedly not into playing 'urchin' music.

If music really was the food of love, then we would have preferred something with chips in our dinner hall, thanks very much. Fat Mary of 2C2, bless her, certainly would have.

26

The chicken crossed the road – once too often

Today glumly pushing a wire trolley, with a mind of its own, through the serried ranks of frozen, fresh, chilled, organic, free-range, battery, butter-basted or 'super-roosters', its easy to forget the days when a chicken was the big event for Christmas. If you could get one, that is.

For obvious reasons during the war we never had much in the way of food, and especially when it came to the butcher's. Our ration was measured in single sausages, scrag-end of mutton or sometimes, with a wink to hang on until the shop was empty, a piece of liver for Dad's tea. Corporal Jones of Dad's Army may be a comic caricature militarily but he was deadly serious as a butcher.

Poultry (and I never actually saw a turkey other than one in an illustrated Charles Dickens novel) was not exactly plentiful until a week or so before Christmas. Then, in a display that would send shudders through a local environment officer today, they would be hung by their scrawny necks all day long outside the shop, or perhaps on a market stall in Petticoat Lane.

Even so they were snapped up very quickly and unless you knew of a black market source (which many people did) the festive season was always preceded by a battle of wits to lay ones hands on a bird. Yes, we did have chickens in the back garden but mainly they were egg-layers and I suspect our few rabbits broke out into cold sweats some Decembers.

Christmas for us kids meant toys out of Woolworths, books, an orange (and you had to get real lucky for one of them) and perhaps a bar of Caley Tray, which was a slab of milk chocolate with six soft centred chocs built into it. For Mum and Dad though the chicken problem was an annual headache, though to be fair they usually managed it somehow. Considering she could only cook chicken once a year the flavour of her roast chicken is something I still remember with mouth-watering ecstasy.

But there was one year when their chicken luck seemed to run out. I think it was about 1944 and though she had the ration points there seemed to be a shortage of the actual birds. The butcher couldn't guarantee getting enough for all his registered customers in by Christmas Eve, and a regular black-market source had been unexpectedly arrested.

I remember Dad going up to Petticoat Lane in desperation to see if he could get a bird on the old 'nudge nudge wink wink' basis but coming back empty handed. It was starting to look like rabbit stew for the 25th - then in the nick of time Uncle Syd arrived home on leave.

Now Uncle Syd, my mother's youngest brother, was a personal hero and not least because he was a sailor. He'd been called up by the admiralty and had done his Russian convoys quota before getting torpedoed in the Med. His ship, the HMS Nigeria, – hadn't sunk but had been badly damaged and many of the crew had been lost. I remember him once coming home on leave with a sailor's uniform he'd made for me – sadly it was too small and I cried my eyes out because I couldn't get it on. Years later I had one of my own to wear and even that one was tight.

Anyway the point was that Syd was a Chatham rating (as I was destined to be one day) so between ships he was billeted in Chatham Barracks and that made it easy to get home. Until he got married he lived with us while on leave and on this occasion he made it to our front door a couple of days before Christmas. More importantly he was concealing a dead chicken in his kitbag.

In those days you had to walk to the station from Chatham Barracks through some leafy lanes and passing some farmyards. It appears he'd been doing that a few hours before on his way home when this chicken suddenly emerged from a farm to cross the road. Before Syd could help this Rhode Island Red back into the farm it had obviously wandered out of, it threw itself into his kitbag, breaking its neck in the process. A kindly man he didn't have the heart to go and break the bad news to the farmer that one of his birds had committed suicide, so had brought it home instead.

In Dagenham he was greeted with open arms of course but when he produced his contribution to the feast as well the old man was so pleased he gave him a bottle of brown ale there and then. I think that bird was plucked, emptied of giblets (did you know they do not come from a plastic bag inside the bird?), was filled with sage and onion and readied for the oven before he'd even drunk his beer. I expect the rabbits were able to relax as well.

Mum did her usual magnificent job and we all smacked our lips in eager anticipation as she began to carve it up. Then we tried to eat it.

That fowl proved to be not only tasteless but so hard and rubbery it was like chewing a Wellington boot. No wonder it had committed suicide – it was probably so old it had nothing left to live for so had crossed that road that day on a poultry Hari Kari mission. It was so tough it even broke dad's denture.

We had rabbit stew on Boxing Day that year

27

No flies on Mrs Morrison

About thirty years ago I did a stint as a school governor and part of my 'duty' was the acceptance of an invitation by the headmaster to enjoy a school dinner with him and the kids. My mind flashed back over the years as it desperately searched for an excuse to turn him down without causing offence, but in the end I had to accept with good grace.

So it came to pass that one morning I arrived in the headmaster's study expecting, and hoping, to be fortified with a pre-lunch sherry or three to help me through the ordeal. In fact I got a quick cup of coffee that wasn't even decaffeinated, before taking a deep breath and following him into the hall to be served.

I got the shock of my life. I found pleasantly smiling dinner ladies doling out portions of chips that looked, and tasted, like chips or ladling out boiled potatoes – real potatoes – obviously edible carrots and peas, to go with succulent meat pie full of steak and kidney simply dripping with gravy. What's more the kids were clamouring for it and shoving each other aside in their eagerness to fill their plates with food.

It made me realise just how much things had changed because my own experiences of school dinners had been quite horrific. In fact our greatest excitement came when the biology block, with our dining hall on the floor above the labs, caught fire one morning and burned to the ground taking that day's dinners with it.

Yes, in the forties and early fifties times were still hard – but so were the peas, pies and puddings they force fed us with in Rosslyn Road and other schools. Not the potatoes – because even our school cooks would have had problems making 'Pom' (mashed potato powder) hard, though when it came to the weekly plate of fish and chips, they invariably succeeded.

The peas often came in useful, once smuggled out of the dinner hall, in terms of playground combat ammunition for our peashooters, but we could have soled our boots with the congealed flour and water that passed as piecrust. That level of petrified pastry was used in two separate courses. In the first it would be smeared with a layer of mysterious brown chunks smelling vaguely of Bovril, to partner a flop of cabbage, a rattle of peas or a scoop of Pom.

When used as part of 'afters' it would come with a layer of unidentified jam, the flavour of which would be stifled by a prodigious pool of runny yellow liquid that passed as custard. Sometimes, as a change, we had sponge pudding, but that was a laugh too because it was so rubbery you could play tennis with it.

I once had an unforgettable experience with Pom. I sat down one lunchtime to look once again at this miserable dollop of white stodge nestling up to the peas and for some reason I prized it apart with my knife and fork. Nestling inside one of the halves was a dead fly which had somehow managed to commit hari-kari in a mixing bowl somewhere down the line.

Stunned, even a little sickened because we'd recently had a biography lesson in which we'd been shown just how dodgy dead flies were in health terms, I just sat and stared at it until I felt a movement by my shoulder. Frau Morrison had arrived.

Mrs Morrison, our German teacher, I have mentioned before. She was a big big lady who, it was rumoured, had fled the Nazis before the war. She had turned up in Rosslyn Road where she did her best to get us speaking her native language, albeit not as well and gutturally as she did. She was feared throughout the school as a strict disciplinarian who other teachers, unable to handle us, would send miscreants to her class for punishment, which meant being beaten up.

She had the knack of standing you next to the wall blackboard and fetching up a right hand clout that made your head bounce onto (and back off) the blackboard. Now she stood by my shoulder glaring down at me. 'Lynch, Vy are you not eating.' She snarled.

'Er, well miss, I seem to have a dead fly in my potato,' I stammered fearfully.

'Vell, take it out put to one side of your plate and get on vith the rest of your food,' she ordered.

Perhaps I forgot to mention - I never did like that woman.

28

The Barking dog 'sang'

There are those who made a big fuss today about what they call 'reality TV' shows – they get lost in jungles with nonentities, watch aspiring young business 'apprentices' stabbing each other in the back or get gripped by Big Brother. The latter is streets away from the Orwellian version, but does appear to contain the same kind of voyeuristic purpose.

I am no fan of either Jungle or Brother, though I must admit to a leaning towards The Apprentice while others, like Strictly Come Dancing and Ready Steady Cook, do come close to compulsive viewing.

You will notice that the ones I do like a little have an entertainment base and since they killed off the big variety shows at least offer a modicum of glamour in their place. Happily they usually also offer it without the kind of foul-mouthed lavatorial claptrap that too often passes for comedy these days.

So why am I going on about this? Well because they remind me of the famous 'singing dog' act that packed a Barking pub (yes, well it had to be there right?) back in the early to mid-fifties. In those days every pub had a music licence and its own local Sinatra or Elvis hammering the eardrums on Friday and Saturday nights. The 'singing dog' though, did sound a bit special and the Mild Bunch decided to give it a whirl.

Now if there was one benefit that National Service did bring it was that if you went into a boozer in uniform, almost everyone in the place was keen to buy your drinks, because they knew how skint you were. In those days we were paid something like the equivalent of £1.40 a week so even though beer was about a shilling a pint, we were never really flush.

At this particular time Ginger B had been demobbed from the army and Buddy was still doing his apprenticeship so I was the only one of us in uniform. This night the uniform did its job well and I was well into the regular line-up of pints provided by regulars by the time the evening's entertainment began.

The pub, I forget its name now but it was in Ilford Lane near to Barking Park, was packed so clearly the fame of the singing dog had spread far and wide, but by half-past nine there was still no sign of the animal. We'd had our eardrums brutalised by the usual 'Frankie and Johnny' renditions, along with the pseudo-American voice of the local Gene Vincent, but we'd all come to see the singing dog, so where was he?

The guy on the microphone had already made a few excuses for the non-appearance when the door opened and a weedy looking bloke with the biggest and scruffiest Irish wolfhound you ever saw on a lead, walked in. To the obvious relief of the regulars he made his way over to the piano with the dog and the audience fell quiet in expectation.

Once settled, he glanced around the pub and his eyes settled on me, resplendent in uniform. 'Good evening everyone, I see we've got the Navy in tonight, so I think we'll start with a tribute to our jolly Jack Tars', he said.

With the dog sitting on its haunches beside him he began to play a medley of old sea shanties – the kind that always went down well in a pub full of drunks, even outside Portsmouth, and in the Last Night of the Proms. He skipped through the 'Sailor's Hornpipe', got our feet tapping with Hearts of Oak, and then he started to play Tom Bowling.

Now this particular song, as all good Promenaders know, is a pretty sad ditty about an ex-shipmate who has just been splashed over the side sewn up in canvas. Not a happy boozing song by any means, but this time instead of just playing it he began to sing the words. Then, as his thin and mournful voice began to drip-feed into our Double Diamond and Red Barrel fed emotions, the dog joined in.

Well, to be honest it wasn't exactly singing – it just threw back its head and started howling like a wolf out on the Canadian timberline. It drowned out his master's voice but stopped howling when he finished the song and that turned out to be their act.

The blasted thing sat quietly as long as he just played the joanna, but once he started to sing we got the full blast of the Call of the Wild and, believe it not, we loved it. To this day I still cannot believe how much we cheered that howling dog in Barking that night.

I guess it was variety and reality, our style.

29

We were all 'gropers' then

At sea I have been tossed around in a 'Bermuda Triangle' hurricane, been violently and physically sick into bilges during a North Sea storm, and broken out into cold sweats hearing huge chunks of ice thudding into the side of the engine room I was working in not far from where the Titanic went down. Even so the worst thing of all was arriving in the English Channel in a blanket of thick fog, with a dozen ships horns sounding off all around us.

That was close to fear, even though we had grown up with that and worse and I don't mean the blitz. I am talking about smog and it took many years and a Clean Air Act to make that a thing of the past. This wasn't just fog, but a real killer. Year after year we groped our way home, gate by gate, from school in thick and grimy blankets of the stuff, relying on memory and guestimates of where we were. A choking sooty fog that hung around for days and in which you really couldn't see your hand in front of your face.

Buses had to be led back to their garages at walking pace with conductors walking in front of them holding flares to guide the driver. No other traffic would be on the road because of the total lack of visibility and this often went on for days at a time with the country virtually paralysed. At home rooms were made as smog proof as possible but this deadly black mist killed thousands, my own gran included, as they struggled for oxygen.

Conan Doyle, and others of his ilk, romanticised the old Victorian 'pea soupers', using them as props to heighten the tension as their villains stalked the gas-lit alleyways of the East End. Could Jack the Ripper have been caught if he hadn't had the comforting blanket of black fog swirling around him as he escaped from the carnage of his latest victim? Even post-war villains had their moments, and such stories about the 'fog felons' used to abound.

Take the guy who, so the story went, decided to fit himself out with a nice new suit from the window of a tailor's shop in Chadwell Heath. Taking advantage of the smog late one wintry night he hurled something heavy through the window, leapt in and grabbed his suit, complete with dummy, before jumping out again and going up on his toes.

Clutching his new clerical grey whistle, complete with dummy, he dashed across the road to make his escape. Sadly he dashed straight into the police car that was cruising slowly, and cautiously, through the smog towards the local nick (and presumably canteen) a hundred yards away. When I say straight into, I do mean with some considerable force.

Naturally the very concerned rozzers leapt out of their motor to see if they could help this road accident victim, and see what damage their motor had inflicted. He was just bruised and shaken, but then they got very interested in the suited dummy he'd been carrying under his arm when they'd whacked into him. They nicked him instead.

The cause of the smog was always very well known. Our world then was a highly industrialised one that relied massively on the burning of coal and coke. It was a boiler-room world where King Coal still ruled, not just in the factories and power stations but in office, hospitals and of course homes as well.

From October onwards millions of homes poured out

their deadly cocktails of sooty and sulphurous smoke, adding to the clouds already being pumped out by industrial chimneys. You could even forecast the weather by the way smoke came out of chimneys – if it floated downwards it was bound to rain. Little wonder then that, in His infinite wisdom God decided too much was floating up to heaven, so decided to send it back down again.

Coal was as essential to us at home as it was to Ford's Foundry but it brought its domestic problems too. As kids a night indoors usually developed into a battle of wits about which one was going to put the kettle on for tea, and who was going out to the coal shed to fill the scuttle up for the evening. There were some good points about those days though.

Toasted bread, for example, (or crumpets) never tasted as good as when held arms length on the end of a long wire fork held over the hot red embers of the fire. The same went for baked potatoes and roast chestnuts. In fact before the advent of television the fireplace used to be the focal point of family life, with the coal scuttle the chore of the night.

Dad in his chair reading the Evening News, or that morning's Daily Herald, with mum in hers, knitting needles clicking away as she created new socks or cardigans for the men and boys in the family. Meanwhile we kids would be sprawled around the hearthrug reading the Wizard or the latest Denis Wheatley, listening to Take it From Here or the Goons on the wireless at the same time.

Today's radiators don't have that kind of appeal, do they? Still at least the smog has gone, so there's no arguments about filling up the coal scuttle. Anyway, in today's hierarchy I have to make the blasted tea anyway.

30

Dudley Moore robbed me

I cannot pretend to have been a bosom pal of Dudley Moore, although we knew each other by sight as fellow members of the Valence House library in the Avenue and lived within a street and a few hundred yards of each other. We chatted occasionally when we both left the library on the way home but there came a day when I hated him.

Now, I have always felt lucky that I grew up in a 'Golden Age' of great comedians. My boyhood show-biz heroes were Robb Wilton and Arthur Askey then, after the war, we had a rich harvest of laughs from comics like 'Ancock, Max Bygraves, the Goons, Frankie Howerd, Benny Hill and of course the greatest clown of them all, Tommy Cooper.

In the cinema we had Norman Wisdom and Laurel and Hardy of course but they were only half British (Stan Laurel). All of them, however could make you helpless with laughter without the slightest hint of a swear word – even the great Max Miller never resorted to profanity. If he told a dirty joke it was only because it was you who interpreted it that way.

I was stage struck and fantasised many an hour of my youth on the stage of the London Palladium, though the best I ever actually managed was a leading role in the 11th Dagenham Scout Gang Show in Lymington Road School. Well apart, that is, from the day Eric Johnson and I went on stage at the Odeon Saturday Morning Cinema Club ('We *come along on Saturday morning - greeting everybody with a smile...la la la')* in the Regent cinema in Green Lane.

Eric and I were regulars, well we all were then, and when they announced a talent contest one week I persuaded him that we should enter as a new Flanagan and Allen double act. He agreed and I worked on a series of one-line jokes, mainly lifted directly from the Hotspur and Wizard, but even when we worked on the routine in my front room it was clear that it never really worked.

I mean, eleven year olds can't really get away with 'that's no lady, that's my wife' kind of jokes. Then, on the Friday night before our appearance, I had an inspiration and changed the act.

The following morning we were introduced on-stage to the rapturous applause of dozens of our own mates, and school friends, packing the first few rows. The new act consisted of me telling a ghost story with Eric behind me doing the sound and visual effects. For example I would speak of someone 'rolling their eyes in horror' and Eric would roll a tennis ball across the stage behind me. I told of the wind whistling through the trees and he would blow a police whistle we'd bought in the Army and Navy Surplus Stores in Green Lane that very morning.

All corny stuff, yeah I know that, but we were a smash. With everyone in the first few rows shouting and clapping their hands for us we stormed through that first heat as clear winners. This was fame and we drank it in.

The following Saturday was the second heat of course and we had to have a new act – another story and more 'effects'. I tell you the demands of our German and Maths homework suffered dearly that week as we sweated blood rehearsing the new story.

Came the day and we were ready, confident and ready for more local stardom. Our nerves jangled as we waited to go on stage but the Palladium, even Hollywood was beckoning, and believe me we were great again even though I say it myself. Our gags were better and our effects even more hilarious and our whole act more sophisticated than it had been the week before. By the end of our turn we were basking in the sunshine of laughter again – so how come we lost?

I will tell you. We were beaten that day by that bloody kid I knew only vaguely from the library but who'd never made me laugh as we'd strolled home together. All he could do was play the piano. Yes ok, he wasn't bad at it though I was a bit surprised to hear Mozart going down so well in our picture house.

What he did have however was more school mates in the front few rows than we had that time. We all smiled sportingly and applauded his success that morning but inside how I hated that boy.

I always felt that Eric and I, certainly me, could have gone on to great things from that talent show. Instead German and Maths prevailed and we gave up the idea of a show business career. The pianist went on to fame, fortune and the Hollywood career I could have had if he hadn't turned up that Saturday morning.

I never spoke to him in the library again.

31

Didn't we have a luverley day

Of course it wasn't always 'Soufend' – sometimes it was Clacton or even 'Margit'. It never really mattered as long as the pubs were plentiful, the bumper cars were bumping and there was an abundance of whelk stalls stretched out along the seafront.

Knowing of my addiction to Del Trotter and Only Fools and Horses one of the kids bought me the Jolly Boys Outing for Christmas and I still get a kick out of watching that coach blow up.

As far as I can see they don't seem to do 'beanos' any more – at least not in the way we did when a collector would be going around the factory for months getting the contributions for the 'big day'.

When it arrived crates of ale would be stowed into the coach just before we all piled aboard. Southend of course is only about thirty miles or so away – but by the time we reached it the pubs would not yet be open. It was a case of a 'lay-by' thirst break to ensure that by the time we did get there we would already have been refreshed and ready for a quick session in the Foresters Arms before hitting the Kurzaal amusement park.

It really was just a boozer's day out, and on such Saturdays Grey-Green Coaches and the other coach companies would be disgorging hordes of husbands, dads and boy friends, free for the day, onto the town's car parks in good time to get the first rounds in. As I say, it wasn't always Southend but it was certainly the most popular venue as far as the East Enders (which Dagenham was full of anyway) were concerned.

Blackpool has its 'Golden Mile' we had our seafood half-mile - small stalls piled high with cockles, mussels and whelks, or little bowls ready to have the juiciest of jellied eels spooned into them to be handed over with a chunk of fresh bread. There they stood, with a raucous backdrop of amusement arcades, the bingo callers shouting out their numbers and the incessant laughter of the 'laughing policeman' rocking about in his glass case. Mr Rossi would be selling his wonderful ice cream in odd spaces along with the 'spieler' pledging that he wasn't going to ask us five quid for a twenty-five piece dinner set.

We had our priorities of course. The pubs closed after lunch in those days, so the revellers needed to ensure they were sufficiently well oiled by then so a few hours snoozing on a deckchair or, for us younger ones, flying high on the big wheel or roundabouts, or simply staggering loudly down the end of the pier just for the hell of it.

Apart from stuffing myself silly with whelks I even have a hazy memory on one beano of joining in a Salvation Army service on the seafront one year. Then, with the clock ticking away we would all straggle our way back to the coach park, in order to ensure we were aboard in time to leave so we could catch opening time at the Half Way House or some other hostelry.

There we would remain for a few hours until, somehow, we would be levered back into the coach and then unceremoniously dumped outside the factory so the driver (who did rather well out of tips from drunks of course) could go back to base and clean his coach out.

Even when we were very small a day out in Southend was about the best our parents could do as far as a holiday was concerned. No booze for us kids then of course but it was where I developed my lifelong addiction to shellfish and my first sight of a drunken granny.

My father, knowing of my growing affection for a bowl of whelks, escorted me from the beach where Mum was looking after brother and sister, across the road to the whelk stalls. We were just about to give our order when he grabbed me by the shirt and hustled me away back across the road. I was puzzled until I saw the reason.

Also heading for the pub and about to pass the whelk stall was a line of drunken old dears clearly on a beano from the East End. They were singing and dancing, having a right old knees-up... and there in the middle of the line, as stoned as the rest, was his mother – Granny Lynch.

32

Nice one Emma

As I write this I am filled with pride for my youngest daughter Emma who, despite the searing heat, completed her first London Marathon in April (2007). I think all those thousands who took part that day deserved their medals but Em was the first in our family to actually go out there and plod along to the Palace to get hers.

Like me she has had several career changes – starting out as a chef, moving into nursing and then becoming a personal trainer in a local gymnasium (her, not me) – but until recent years she never really showed a great deal of enthusiasm for running.

Well, perhaps not strictly true – as a youngster she would run a mile whenever there were chores like washing up to be done, though to be fair her siblings usually moved much quicker than she did. In my own case PT (physical training) was something we all did with reluctance and especially so in the winter when we boys were expected to strip to the waist in the playground to do some ridiculous arm and leg bending exercises.

We never played a lot of cricket at school because the summer holidays used to stretch out over the season, but football was always a passion. (I even played a couple of games for Dagenham's 'A' team before the government insisted on press-ganging me for a couple of years to do National Service.) There was one school event though that some of us dreaded even more than the annual Sports Day when we were expected, required even, to sprint, jump, leap about a bit and plod a mile.

This was the annual 'cross-country' run through some woods in Chigwell and for which we were all, the entire school, volunteered. They bussed whole classes to Chigwell for an event which was mapped out through the woods, beginning at one end and emerging from the other. It was a six-mile test which took the runners way out into the countryside before coming back into the forest to head out across the final field to the finish.

Now in a sense this was a bit of a result for me because, as it happened, I knew those woods very well. It was a favourite picnic spot my mother was very fond of, as well as being a bit of an adventure place for us kids, including the Mild Bunch. For just the cost of a bus ticket and a bottle of lemonade powder dissolved in water we could spend all day out in the fresh air, climbing trees a long way from the avenue.

I seem to recall that there were four or five of us on the Great Run Scam one year. Over a hundred kids started together with some of us ensuring we was the last bunch to enter the cover of the woodland with the rest of the field already beginning to stretch out before us. Once the coast was clear, we dived into some convenient bushes and waited until everything was quiet.

Then still well concealed by the trees, we ambled up towards the point where the trees broke cover again for the winning 100 yards. There we settled down for a quiet fag as we waited for our group to reappear. Eventually they came into sight so once the first group had passed us we came out of the undergrowth and rejoined the race.

Then, with a great deal of theatrical puffing and panting, we made a dash for the line. I guess we came in about fourteenth or fifteenth, to the applause of the watching teachers and other non-participants. We got the points for our 'House' (Abbey in my case) and for an hour or so revelled in our new status as great cross-country runners.

It all came unstitched though. Vic Hamilton, our sports master, knowing of our usual reluctance to spend energy on pointless running, got very suspicious as he saw us breast the tape with our great 'Oscar winning' displays of glory. Then, as all the other runners came in behind us, his suspicions were confirmed and he began to ask us some pretty pointed questions about our route.

It all finished up with a kind of steward's enquiry supervised by the headmaster, which took the points away from us and replaced them with a week's detention. I mean, how were we supposed to know that part of the approved route had taken the runners through a deep muddy field? We were the only runners to arrive back with pristine white plimsolls and mud-free socks. Bit of a dead giveaway actually.

Still at least Emma never cheated – well it was all on the telly so she couldn't, could she?

33

Punchups in the playground

Whatever side of the playground you were kicking a ball about in, you always knew when some 'bovver' was in the offing. The playground telegraph sent its shouted ' *fight – fight'* signal, and there would be a concerted rush towards the action.

Embryonic Stanley Matthews and Tom Finneys would pick up the tennis balls they had been dribbling with to make a beeline for the action. They would be almost killed in the rush as the girls dropped their skipping ropes and rushed to the scene screaming for blood as they jostled for a ringside place.

The crowd would gather around the two young 'toughs', who were already at the *'Yeah? Yeah!'* stage and circling each other as they muttered their challenges and matching responses of' *'Come on then, why doncha try it'* – *'Nah, you first'*. (Oh yes we had polished repartee in Stevens Road).

Suddenly, as each of the protagonists realised no teacher was handy enough to rescue them by breaking up the eyeball to eyeball confrontation, they hurled themselves at each other. What followed would be a succession of grunts, groans and muttered threats as the pair wrestled each other to the ground. Gang mates would be roaring one or the other on while girls would be squealing and shrieking their encouragement to both.

This was urchin conflict - the asphalt jungle at its rawest.

On the gravel the pair would roll round and round, each trying to grab the other's wrists in an attempt to protect himself from a punch in the eye. (Black eyes took longer to heal than bloody noses.) One of the warriors would generally finish up on top and, sitting astride his opponent – but then he realised he had a new problem.

If he released one wrist so that he could whack his victim, he stood more than an even chance of getting biffed himself. He was forced to hold both his opponent's arms down while he thought about it. Actually, to the frustration and disappointment of the alleged gentle sex, usually there was very little blood – but there was always a lot of noise and many grazes, as naked knees raked along the gravel.

In fact the decibel level would reach such a peak that eventually the duty teacher, sitting in the staff room enjoying her cuppa, realised she (most of our teachers were female because the blokes were away in the army), had a problem to sort out. Angrily she would sally forth to push her way through the multitude of screeching playgrounders.

There she would grab the top miscreant by the scruff of his neck and the grounded one by his jacket and jerk them apart to march inside. Then it was a case of being parked outside the head teachers study waiting in trepidation – made worse by the threat of the 'slipper' - when she called us in to mete out justice.

Yes, we grew up in an environment of violence with bombsites and the debris of war everywhere to remind us of what was going on around us; but our personal wars had little to do with 'itler. Put it down to juvenile male macho, nourished by parents who refused to listen to complaints about being bullied and simply told you to go back to school and next time get the first punch in.

Protests that the bully was bigger brought even less comfort. *'Well, you've got boots, haven't you?'*

To be honest boot fights were rare. Like our comic book

heroes, Rockfirst Rogan, Biggles and the rest, we fought fists with fists never with the boot and certainly never with knives. Well, ok, boots as a last resort if we were getting the worst of it.

It was a hard, rough and tough world for us boys, while for the girls it was a case of waiting demurely, skipping and playing hopscotch or other girlie games until playtime was over.

Well, until the word went round that there was a fight on and they could grab their ringside seat, screech for their boy friend and bay for blood from either.

34

The devil galloped every night

I remember it clearly. I was bored stiff on the A12 one summer's afternoon on my home when it came over the radio and the car was filled with a musical memory that transported me back over sixty years. Suddenly I was back on the carpet in front of the fire, a doorstep slab of bread smeared with damson jam clutched in my hands, listening with wondrous anticipation as the man said the words... *'Dick Barton - Special Agent!'*

At that moment, 6.45pm Monday to Friday, a million kids and more nationwide would be yelling in excitement, barely able to wait for the 'Devil's Gallop' to finish, so we would be able to find out how our hero had just escaped certain death the previous night.

Nowadays the slot is filled (I believe) by The Archers, which started after Barton had been consigned to history; but for us it was a non-adult quarter hour packed with high drama and sound effects to make you dribble for. In later years of course we nurtured another 'secret agent' by the name of Bond, but our nightly (with an 'omnibus edition' on Saturday when they managed to squeeze five quarter hours into a single hour) was our fix then.

After all we'd been arguing about him all that day in the playground – speculating on how he'd managed to get out of his current scrape, knowing full well of course that he would. How would he, and/or his sidekicks Jock and

Snowy, manage to get out of the car crash or escape the descending ceiling threatening to crush them flatter than a hedgehog on the Great North Road?

These were the days when a mobile phone was the stuff of science fiction, along with computers, hovercraft and colour TV. Dick Barton was a 'special agent' though no one seems to have been quite sure which of our British institutions he was working for, except that it was always against international criminal masterminds.

Once the magic words had been spoken on the Light Programme we were knee-deep in terrorists, crooks, scoundrels and master criminals - all doing their best to damage our hero. DB saw off the perils of ray guns, deadly plagues and many fiendish ways of despatching not just him but all humanity.

We never really needed a cinematic pyrotechnician to produce spectacular volcanoes or fiery explosions – the BBC had a marvellous sound effects department who knew their job. So in that precious fifteen minutes of fantasy Dick, Snowy and Jock would rescue each other, be beaten to a pulp and find themselves back in dead lumber again by 7pm, by which time an exhausted sound effects man was presumably ready for bed.

At that time, as another movement of the Devils Gallop music began to home in, we'd be hearing....'Can Dick? Will Jock? Or, is it the end for Snowy?' leaving us in suspense and in line for more playground punch-ups the next day.

One thing you never did hear from Barton, or even his enemies, was a swear word. Perhaps the most daring 'expletive' was cockney Snowy's occasional 'Crikey', though the other clichés ring down the years. 'Look out, he's got a gun', 'Oh no you don't chum, take that!' Nor did our hero ever have a girl friend, though he did of course rescue the occasional token heroine who was never heard of again.

They did try to make a Dick Barton film of course and we all packed into the Regent in Green Lane to see it. It proved to be an amateurish disaster that proved once again the supremacy of the radio sound effects man. Will they ever bring Barton back? Can he find Jock and Snowy in time? Can they escape from the exploding mineshaft?

Crikey, of course they did!

35

Bring back those old time socialists

I love elections. I have reported on them, been telly-eyed through the night many a time, and even stood in (and won) them myself, but I guess you never forget your first. It's only in later years, when hurtful jokes about being able to tell when politicians are lying (because their lips are moving), that the reality becomes tinged with cynicism.

I wasn't even ten when I took part in my first campaign. It was June 1945 and the Mild Bunch was just getting used to being able to play football and cricket in the park without having to dive for cover. A month or so earlier Dad had called my brother and I in from the street to hear the familiar growl of the 'prime minister' declaring that the war was over.

I can still see Mum, Dad, and Granny Lacey who lived with us, that day with tears in their eyes as they raised tiny glasses of sherry to 'peace', muttering 'good ole Winnie'. This was particularly odd as far as Dad was concerned, because he was a belt and braces, lifelong socialist and totally committed trades unionist. Yet there he stood, toasting the Tory leader who he both admired and despised. He was very quick to help vote him out.

I am the first these days to acknowledge the massive debt that we owe to Clement Attlee and his radical Labour government, but I couldn't understand it at the time. We worshipped Churchill (I still do to be honest) and for him to get dumped out of office was something we kids never quite understood at the time. There were, of course, good historical reasons, but we never knew that.

Yet suddenly, and without quite knowing how or why, we kids were marching down the street in our short trousers with hanging underpants, singing, *'Vote, vote, vote for Mr Ranger* (who was Labour's candidate in our end of Ilford) *and kick old Churchill in the eye. If it wasn't for the King we would do the (expletive deleted) in'*

On the other side of Bennetts Castle Lane – the Dagenham side which was lit at night by gas lampposts – they were singing to vote, vote, vote for John Parker. I have no idea where we got the words from, or who taught us to sing it.

These were the days when the Labour Party was full of real socialists – men and women with dirt or soapsuds under their fingernails – rather than the wealthy lawyers, accountants and professional politicians who have hijacked it since. I can't quite see any more Tessa Jowells or Margaret Hodges emerging from the ranks of the office cleaners or laundry workers, and where are the ex-miners, electricians and railwaymen?

I am not sure where some MPs get their politics from these days. In 1945 we had politicians of conviction through personal experience – now we have many who should be convicted for personal excesses. How many of today's alleged socialists, for example, could hold a candle to the legendary John Parker who held Dagenham for so many years without so much as a hint of scandal attached to him?

How many members of Blair's or Brown's cabinets had the persuasive skills and background of Nye Bevan, or the sheer political dedication of Manny Shinwell (who once lived in Ilford by the way)? They were men of integrity who knew what a day's work really was, having learned their lessons at the coal face.

As a one-time member of the Labour Party I find it all very sad. I am also very positive that the most genuine socialist I ever knew – my TGWU bus driver, father - would be horrified at what has been done to the legacy of 1945.

I certainly am!

36

So where did I go wrong?

In my first book of reminiscences (In My Own Lynchtime) I wrote that the Ilford, Dagenham and Barking I grew up and was educated in, was a crucible of talent. We didn't realise it then of course - the only big local hero in those days was a full back called Alf Ramsey who, sadly, played for Spurs and not West Ham. I often wonder what happened to him.

We raked the streets in full ragamuffin kit – stained pullovers, torn jackets and short trousers with hanging underpants – shoplifting in Woolworths, or playing football and cricket in the parks. Between streaming to the Saturday Morning Pictures, midweek we waited outside the cinemas begging adults to take us in if there was an 'A' movie on. (You can just see parents letting that happen these days).

Yet, while we never knew it of course, future show business stars, footballers, millionaires and even an Archbishop of Canterbury, were growing up among us. They were probably jostling to get in front of us on Saturday mornings as we waited to get into the Regent and challenging us to football 'kickabouts' over the park after school.

A couple of years ago I wrote the biography of one of them – a certain John Bairstow who grew up in Ilford. Five years older than me, he'd run away to sea, fought with the Gloucesters on the Imjin River and then founded two major companies - Bairstow Eves and the Queens Moat Houses hotel chain.

One of his friends and colleagues in the estate agency was Alan Cherry out of Chadwell Heath, who went on to found Countryside Properties. Another future developer called Don Moody lived on the opposite side of the Avenue to me. He left school to become a bricklayer and I remember my father advising me that that was no sort of job for a young man, labouring on the building sites in all sorts of weather. So Don finished up owning Moody Homes, and made a few quid.

Show business – well there was always Dudley Moore around the corner in Baron Road. We had a nodding acquaintanceship in the library, but my cousin Joan told me that she only started going to Sunday School after she found out he was in the choir at nearby St Thomas's church. He also did me out of a show biz career (see reminiscence 30)

There were other local stars who'd already emerged. During the war young Vera Lynn from Barking did quite well as a singer and 'Forces Sweetheart', while Oscar winner Greer Garson (Mrs Miniver) came out of Ilford, as did another future alleged celebrity called Noel Edmonds though that was much later and even after us of course.

Mentioning Dudley and the church brings to mind names like Cardinal John Heenan, who was born in Ilford but was a Manor Park parish priest at the time I was nicking cheap toys out of Woolies, but Dagenham had its own religious star in the making then. That was in the shape of young Georgie Carey, who emerged from our rain-washed streets to become Archbishop of Canterbury, and is now Lord Carey.

But for most of us kids, rainless and school-free days and evenings were spent kicking footballs around in Valence Park. There we would do our best to end the careers of the likes of Jimmy Greaves and Terry Venables (Bonham Road)

– a scamp I remember well. Nipper Venables had too much energy, and skill, for us older teenagers who would flop down for a quick rest while he chased a loose ball kicked up to the far end of the park.

In those days snooker was something dodgy blokes played in seedy halls above the Fifty-bob Tailor's shops, but the guy who really made it a front line TV event was another Chadwell Heath scallywag called Barry Hearn. Like me the son of a bus driver, Barry became an accountant but then he met a young Steve Davis and the rest is history.

So you can see what I meant when I claim I grew up in a crucible of talent. From it came men and women who made history, created fortunes, thrilled and entertained hundreds of thousands, and preached many a sermon from the top of their mountain. They were the sons and daughters of ordinary working people, who went to the same schools I did, probably shoplifted in the same shops we nicked biscuits from and eventually got rich.

So where did I go wrong?

37

A little 'levver' shop in Romford

There used to be a little shop in Victoria Road, Romford that the family called 'the levver shop' because it was where Dad used to buy the 'levver' he used to mend our boots with.

To be honest the old man was a better bus driver than a cobbler. His fingers were too thick to hold those tiny 'tack' nails without whacking his finger, but he could sail past bus queues with all the panache of a regular London Transport 'chauffeur'.

In those days the working classes were 'DIY-ers' long before the term was invented to make B&Q a fortune. Granny Lacey, who lived with us, specialised in knitting and darning socks, sitting by the fire for hours with her triangle of metal needles click-clacking away. From them would descend a good supply of socks for us boys to wear out, and which she would then sit and darn until she was darning the darning. Then, once beyond repair they would be unravelled and the wool used to knit more 'almond rocks' as our Cockney old man called them.

The trips to the levver shop also gave us kids the chance to see the market when it really was a cattle market. We thrilled to the sound of pigs squealing as their ears were clipped, and watched the cows as they thumped down the ramps of the trucks that had brought them, and then up again to who knows where. All to a cacophony of shouting auctioneers and barrow-boys, cackling geese, clucking chickens and the moaning of mournful sheep - part of a scene that would probably horrify so many today.

I remember that little shop with its counter piled high with oddly shaped off cuts of leather in all colours and thicknesses. It also sold other boot mending gear, like 'cobblers lasts', hammers, nails and of course ' blakeys', those metal studs that were used to make repairs last. The whole shop had a wonderful smell and an atmosphere of its own like no other shop had.

Dad would rummage amongst it all until he pulled out a leather off cut he decided was thick enough and big enough for a few soles, and perhaps the odd heel as well. He would buy enough of those small nails to restock the rusty Old Holborn tin he kept his nails in and completed his purchases with a small stick of black 'heelball'.

A few days later he would grab our boots (longer wearing footwear than shoes of course), and sit down on the floor with his cobblers last and a couple of sheets of the Daily Herald to protect the lino. Then, having roughly marked out the shapes he wanted with a pencil, he would cut them out with his very sharp knife.

A boot would be mounted on the last with one of the cut out rough soles on top of it, waiting to be hammered in with series of whacks, bangs and expletives as his fingers and thumb paid a heavy price for being too big. Patiently he would nail it down to the original boot sole, using as many nails as he could hit without bruising himself further.

That done, he would trim the new sole to better fit the shape of the boot, whack in the metal blakeys and studs designed to make the sole (or heel) last longer and which meant we sounded like the fifth act from Lullaby of Broadway whenever we ran anywhere. He'd finish the job by putting a hot poker to the heelball to smear a layer of that waxy grease around the sole to make it waterproof.

That too had its dangers, because if the heelball had been used to often there was the risk of burn blisters on the fingers too.

Job done, he ran his fingers inside to make sure the nails hadn't come through and were waiting for our soft feet to descend on them. In fact I guarantee that we'd be limping in pain in a week anyway as a sharp one came through the levver.

38

A nice quiet Sunday

Tony Hancock once delivered one of the funniest lines ever heard on steam radio when he raged about Hattie Jacques' cooking compared to his mum's. 'At least her gravy used to move about a bit', he told Hattie during one of the most memorable 'Hancock's Half Hours'.

Writers Galton and Simpson really hit the button when they wrote that episode about a typical Sunday afternoon. With Sid James and Bill Kerr (as well as Hattie of course as their housekeeper), Tony captured all the zest and excitement of an afternoon when after the pubs, off licences and newspaper shops closed, so did Great Britain.

There was no television, certainly no cinemas, and all we could get on the wireless was Down Your Way, or Wilfred Pickles 'Have a Go!' – with both shows having all the legendary excitement of watching paint dry. Apart from watching the flies committing suicide on the flypaper hanging from the ceiling, it was a few hours of yawns, snores, repeated requests to know the time, and fascinating games of trying to see imaginary shapes in the wallpaper patterns.

There was of course always the News of the World fashion competitions, but you could never get hold of the paper until after lunch when Dad had dozed off. It was a period of total inertia, made even worse on a rainy day when the only sound apart from the snoring, was the click-clack of Granny Lacey's knitting needles as she knocked out sock after sock.

It would only be relieved when, after an equally boring teatime, we would finally be able to get Variety Bandbox on the wireless, with young Frankie Howerd as its new and upcoming resident comedian.

The front end of the day wasn't a lot better either. Apart from the occasional noisy march past of the Boys Brigade Band, or the concertinas and tambourines of the Salvation Army meeting in the street, the only real distractions came from passing Spitfires, by then being phased out having done their magnificent job.

It was only in later years that I appreciated just why our mother insisted on us going to the Methodist Sunday School around the corner in Haydon Road. Since she was an alleged Church of England 'casual Christian' girl, married to a lapsed and totally disinterested Catholic cockney, it was a bit surprising. What it really meant of course that she had an hour or so peace and quiet – and a regular supply of scent cards. What it meant for us kids was that we knew Twinkle Twinkle Little Star backwards.

We were in our teens before the cinemas realised they had a gold mine on their hands, if only they could persuade the authorities to let them open on Sundays. When they did get permission what they provided was a regular diet of old black and white Jimmy Cagney and Bob Hope films. I think I saw more of Casablanca than Bogart did.

A few years later, when evening television became more available, Jimmy, Bob and Bing etc had yet another new lease of life when the BBC ran old their old films again. Mind you, Sunday evening television started at 7.30pm then with What's My Line, followed by a play in which the crowd scenes were provided by the sound effects man.

Still Hancock was right about one thing. When our mum cooked Sunday lunch, her gravy used to move about a bit as well – quite a lot actually.

39

Confession is good for the sold

Generally speaking journalists are honest folk whose integrity means a great deal to them. They would, for example, no more steal other writer's work than nick their cars. There are morals involved here, standards of decency, honesty and all that - and if you believe that, then I am the Archbishop of Canterbury.

The fact is that if we are unable for some reason (too drunk perhaps) to research a particular topic we have been asked to write a feature on, then would you believe some journalists actually take someone else's article on the same topic and do a rewrite job on it. Then they will add their own by-line and, if they get a result, cheerfully bask in the warmth of editorial praise.

How do I know? Well, partly because I have been involved in journalism now for over forty years and partly because my own experience of committing plagiarism was at the age of ten. To make that even more shameful, in retrospect, I was a Wolf Cub in the 11th Dagenham pack at the time and committed it for our magazine… and a tanner.

I had always fancied my chances as a writer – right from the first time I curled up on our settee with Enid Blyton. If I am to be honest that enthusiasm was mostly fuelled by the realisation that sports reporters got to see West Ham play for nothing. There was also the problem that when it came to other subjects, like maths for example, I was about as useful as a luminous sundial. I had also won a Sunday School prize for an essay 'wot I wrote'.

In fact my brother Roy and I spent some years arguing the toss with our parents about whether we should even go to the Methodist Sunday School round the corner. He was a lapsed and cynical Catholic who was excommunicated for marrying a Protestant, while she was an indifferent CofE without really knowing what that meant.

Anyway, the story of how Brian won a Temperance Essay prize became family legend, and Mum kept that certificate for years, bringing it out to show relatives during brown-ale fuelled Christmas parties. All that however, pales into insignificance compared with my first payment for an article in the 11th Dagenham Scout and Cub magazine. Compared with today's publications it was a very basic job, typed out and copied on a Gestetner machine, but our Scoutmaster pledged to pay a tanner (sixpence) for any article that appeared in it.

I handed in a very nice six or seven verse poem about a boy flying his kite in the park and I even included a pencil drawing of him doing it. To be honest it wasn't a bad piece of poetry and it gave me a buzz to see my first by-line in print for the very first time. That brought an even bigger one when I got my tanner.

The thing was, I hadn't actually written it and anyone who has ever seen a drawing of mine would know that I've got about as much artistic talent as a left handed ant-eater. With hours to go before articles had to be submitted I'd panicked.

Quite shamelessly, in an act that BP would have been appalled at, I plundered the poem from a boy's book I'd had for Christmas. I even scrounged some greaseproof paper from mum to trace the drawing too.

I almost slipped up though. An hour before submission time I realised I had even copied the poet's name as well as his rhyme, putting it in instead of my own. That problem was solved with a slip of paper smeared on one side with some condensed milk and my name written on the other.

Of course I regret it now but it's too late to apologise to the original poet – and anyway the money was spent long ago on a Caley Tray and a bottle of Tizer.

INTERMISSION

The sea urchin

While I have referred to some brief reminiscences of it in this book I spent some of my happiest years at sea. To be fair some of them were reluctant years because of the notion by the governments of the day that lads of my age should help defend my country by being 'press-ganged' (in my case into the navy) for a couple of years doing National Service. I was dragged away at a very early age – well I was 19 actually – from the rain-washed streets of Dagenham to go down to the sea in ships. The urchin was to become a sea-urchin.

H M S Raleigh

On December 6th, 1954 I had my first sight of HMS Raleigh - the 'brick battleship' in Torpoint, just a ferry ride from Plymouth. Along with a few dozen other young bucks I saw it from the back of the naval truck which had picked us up at the railway station and which had delivered us into our National Service.

It had been weeks since I'd received the invitation from Her Majesty that I might like to pop along to her Wanstead medical centre, get myself checked out and sit the 'exams' that would determine the general direction of my life for the next couple of years. Then, having been 'grabbed, groped and coughed', on a medical assembly line of nervous and self-conscious semi-naked teenagers, we had been tested to see if we had any brains at all. Somewhat cynically, we were then asked for our military preferences, as if that made much difference in most cases.

Having watched the RAF in action over their heads as they grew up, most of the lads said they wanted to do their two years in it - and were promptly shoved into the army of course. Some of us, on the other hand, had been deemed intelligent enough and/or had had sufficient family connections (like a couple of uncles who had also served - including a distant one who hadn't reported back after Jutland and another who had done his Russian convoys stint) to be of interest to the Admiralty which never took a lot of national servicemen usually.

I was about to become Stoker Lynch, C/K946568, and spend a couple of years wearing what was then still considered to be the best bird-pulling gear on the dance-floor, and learning how to sink Russian warships. Just to emphasise their keen and urgent need for my services they even sent a railway travel warrant.

By the time the train reached Plymouth that day some of us had got to know each other in the station and train bars. It was all pretty obvious, by our age and suitcases, where we were going even though not all of us were headed for the same uniform. Most were prospective khaki jobs getting off at various points along the line, but a few of us were headed for Plymouth - and HMS Raleigh.

Being quick on the uptake - having been proved intelligent and all that at Wanstead - we guessed that the blue truck waiting at the station with the big white letters RN emblazoned on its doors, probably had something to do with us. Just in case we hadn't guessed there was also a rather loud chap, wearing a peaked cap and dark suit with brass buttons, to emphasise the point. Brandishing a clipboard in his hand he was soon inviting us, in some quite noisy and fairly intemperate language, to climb up into the back of his truck rather quickly.

Chucking our suitcases (which we had been told to bring so we could send our civvies home) we clambered aboard and, I suppose to add to the mystery of the tour, the end flap was closed behind us leaving us all cramped and hanging on for dear life. We were all still making silly nervous jokes about only two years to demob etc, as our 'chauffeur' was hurling his truck through the back streets of Plymouth (Devon) in the general direction of what was presumably Torpoint (Cornwall).

Eventually it stopped, the back flap was ripped open and there was Petty Officer Loudmouth again - still being very offensive - shouting and hollering at us to get down and line up. Clearly it was best to humour him, and most of us almost fell out of the truck in our anxiety to please.

We found ourselves just inside the gates of HMS Raleigh, in front of a guardroom which had two rather attractive little cannons decoratively placed on each side and a flagpole, which was flying the white ensign. We would soon learn to salute these guns whenever we passed them, either on our way into or out of Raleigh.

P.O. Loudmouth, having gained our attention and got us into some kind of straggly order, now noisily explained that he would be our mother and father for the next few months. In the course of his harangue he implied that he himself had not had such benefits, presumably having been born out of wedlock.

Clearly he was already having a bad hair day and meeting us hadn't done much to improve his mood. He prowled up and down our ragged lines, stopping here and there to make some sarcastic remark at one or another of us. We were all dreading him stopping in front of us and, inevitably, he stopped in front of me.

'*Wherejewcomefrom?*' he bawled in my face. I stammered that I was from London, and that seemed to make him even more uptight.

'Wot you doin' ere, then? Wot do you know about ships and the sea dahn there in the Smoke? At least some of these others come from seaside towns', he snarled.

Now in the course of the next few months we learned a great deal, and one of those things was to keep schtumm when faced with such questions. Me, I had to go and reply. '*Been to Ramsgate on me olidays, sir'*, I mumbled - I thought he was going to have a fit.

'*Sir? Sir?*' he shrieked, '*Listen you lot - I ain't no bloody 'Sir'. I am your worst nightmare, a cow-son, a 'shit' of the first order. I am a Petty Officer. You do not salute me - and you do not call me, bloody sir, but you do whatever I bloody well tell you to do. Is that clear?*' he screamed the last few words, but at least he was screaming them to all of us, and no longer homing in on yours truly.

That was only the start. For the next few weeks - they actually sent us home on leave in uniform (bless 'em) for Christmas - PO Loudmouth was true to his word, and worked hard to make our lives a total misery. He marched us in the snow from dawn to dusk, with battered old wartime rifles, teaching us the rudiments of 'drill', in slow time, normal and - more often than not – '*on the double'*. Having supervised the issue of our kit he insisted on having it all laid out in proper order, according to the official diagram, every day. He had us swilling out the toilets (heads) before lights out, and sent us to the barbers so many times a week he must have been copping more backhanders than Tim Henman.

There were others also involved in making our stay in Torpoint memorable of course, and the dentist was one. In those days I grew my own teeth although, having been turned off dentists by the experiences of the school dentist, admittedly they were not in the best of condition,

The Navy of course insisted that we should all have good teeth and thus we all had the usual 'open wide' inspections as soon as we arrived. All seemed well until one day, PO Loudmouth called me out of parade and told me to report to the dentist who, having perused the results of my dental exploration, had expressed a desire to see me. I was not best pleased at this.

In fact by the time I got to the dentist surgery I was pretty wound up about the whole thing. I walked in and (me and my big mouth again) demanded to know of the dentist why he wanted me. In hindsight I realise that I couched this request in the most inappropriate way, and he went spare!

He was, as he explained at length, an officer and the likes of me did not speak to officers in the way I had. He shouted at me and ordered me to sit in his chair. The gist of his outburst was that it was my duty to just do as I was told and not to question officers' motives. I had a filling which needed doing and that is what I was going to get whether I (liked it or not.

I have to admit he did a good job on the filling because it lasted for many years. My only regret at the time though was that, had I been a bit more respectful towards an officer, he might have given me something to deaden the pain instead of using cold steel to practise his arts on my dodgy molar.

Which is why, whenever I see the word Raleigh my mind goes back to that day, that poor parentless Petty Officer and a vicious dentist.

Serving on the Gay Boats

Every ex national serviceman says it never did him any harm, but while he was doing it he wasn't usually in that frame of mind. Many of the lads my age saw active service in the army and RAF in places they probably had never heard of a few years before their call-up. Some of them were killed or maimed in the jungles of Malaya or in places like Cyprus, Kenya and we should not forget Korea either.

I wrote the biography of former estate agent and hotelier John Bairstow who did his National Service in Korea in the fifties and fought with the Glosters in the famous battle on the Imjin River. He survived it but many NS soldiers didn't come home from Korea. My own brother, Roy, did his time in the army in Cyprus though, fortunately without coming to harm.

But I got lucky. I fell into a job in the navy that many would have given their eyeteeth for – I became part of an MTB 'ferry crew', though this was nothing like the Woolwich Free Ferry.

After we got back from our Christmas leave, we had all the prospect of finishing our basic training learning to be 'stokers' at HMS Raleigh, but then they asked for volunteers for a special course on internal combustion engines. The attraction was that this meant being drafted to an old Cunard liner (the Alaunia) which was moored up the river from Devonport, so we could leave Raleigh behind us. We all volunteered and three of us – Lenny 'Swede' Broadhurst from Colchester, Harry Willard, who was older than us because he'd done his training as an architect, and me – were accepted.

The Alaunia was little more than a big empty shell containing living accommodation for those on the actual course. She was tied up alongside an old French destroyer called Dunquerque, and a flat bottom gun monitor, which housed the classrooms, and the NAAFI bar.

So, for the first time, we were living and working with real sailors – some of them with considerable sea time in fact. We slept in hammocks (learning by experience not to tie them for sleeping using a convenient bow that could be pulled apart by some drunken reveller coming back inboard while we were asleep in them). We experienced real shipboard living and mess-deck catering.

I also fell into a dream job without even asking. One of

the crew of the Captain's motor boat had failed to come back from leave because he was sick and for some obscure reason I was allocated to it while we waited for the course to start. Of course it meant lounging around the mess-deck most of the day, waiting for the call for the Captain's motor boat crew to man their boat, but someone had to do it.

When we did finish the course we national servicemen came top of the class and were deemed fit to operate real diesel and petrol engines. That was when I found out that the ones who came lower down the list were drafted to aircraft carriers and the like, while we could be sent to either Coastal Forces (Motor Torpedo Boats) or submarines. Now, to be honest, the idea of being a submariner never really appealed so I was quite relieved when Lenny, Harry and I all got drafted together to HMS Hornet in Gosport to serve in the MTB squadrons. In fact we three did all our two years together.

We found we were to be part of the 'Sixth Ferry Crew' – a team which travelled to different shipbuilders throughout the UK to pick up new MTBs. Then we would bring them back to Gosport, work them up by doing their trials and hand them over to the squadrons while we went and picked up another boat. It was a brilliant little number, and no mistake, though there was one little drawback not obvious or expected at the time.

There was a class of Motor Torpedo Boats (MTBs) that they called the 'Gay' boats because they had names like Gay Bombardier, Gay Charger and the like. These were in the days before the word was hijacked to mean something entirely other than happy of course, but for some time I walked around Portsmouth with the words 'Gay Cavalier' emblazoned across my cap.

All in all, HMS Hornet proved to be a pretty good draft compared to what it could have been and although the only foreign place we ever visited in my Royal Navy time was Caen in France, we did see a lot of British pubs.

The French thing is worth mentioning because we were sent there on a courtesy visit to mark the tenth anniversary of the Normandy landings at Arromanche, near Caen. We were assured we were popular in the town because it had been the British who had liberated Caen. What they neglected to tell us that before D-Day the RAF flattened the place, so we were not all God's chosen people with everyone there.

Even worse, we went there with a submarine which was ordered home after three days because its drunken crew went berserk in Caen. They had to be brought back almost en masse by the local French police one night.

Perhaps it is time now to cut to the chase and remember my last couple of weeks in the Navy – days when I spent my 21st birthday in a coalhole and finished up as 'Engineer Mechanic Harrison'.

Thank God for Engineer Mechanic Harrison
Some moments stick in your mind for ever, and when Dearly Beloved and I popped into the old Chatham Dockyard one Easter some years ago, what came back to me with crystal clarity was the one when I found myself staring up at an enraged naval officer, pointing my own rifle at me.

In fact, had it not been for 'Engineer Mechanic Harrison', instead of celebrating the end of my two years National Service I could have served an extended version of if by spending an uncomfortable Christmas in a military prison.

Most of my service had been spent swanning up and down the coast in MTBs, such as the unforgettable Gay Cavalier, but it was cold sweats all round when the Suez war started in the autumn of 1956. Why? Because it was only weeks before I was due to be demobbed and we were held over pending what happened. Suddenly the Suez Canal had two armies - one Israeli and the other Egyptian - on each bank, and the possibility of racing up and down the canal between them, on tanks of high octane, did not appeal.

However, it all blew over and Harry, Lenny and me arrived back in Chatham's HMS Pembroke, to be demobbed within the fortnight. That was due on the day after my 21st birthday, which in those days was the 'key of the door' day, when you officially became an adult and could even vote, as well as die for your country.

Now anyone who did their bit in the Navy (and I supposed the other services too) knows that you don't just walk out of the gates like that - you have to be 'booked out' of a dozen different departments. So they issue you with a 'draft chit', which is a kind of 'skivers' licence that lets you spend days strolling round getting yourself rubber stamped out of service life. While we waited for that magic piece of paper to be handed over however, we were press ganged into Pembroke's workforce.

This was in November - I was due to be unleashed back onto the Palais circuit on my birthday on the 22nd - and it was pretty nippy weather wise. So seeing my name listed for a boiler house working party did seem like a bit of a result. Although we were called Engineer Mechanics by that time we were still seen as 'Stokers' by some.

Even so, we were still a bit surprised when we reported, to be handed shovels before being marched off to the boiler house. In fact the only coke we would be shovelling was outside in the very chilly fresh air, rather than inside a nice warm boiler room. To this day I can hardly believe what happened.

Chatham barracks was full of little boiler houses, but not all of them had piles of coke to burn - in fact most were not even operational. We were marched to one of those and ordered to bag the pile of coke that lay outside it. Naturally that took us most of the day. Well, little diversions like lunch and the rum issue took up some of the time, but we were in no hurry anyway. We filled the sacks we'd brought with coke onto a barrow and were directed to lug it round to another boiler house at the other end of the barracks. There we emptied them all out into a pile again, and marched off for an evening's revelry in a Chatham boozer, content we had done a good days work.

The next morning we were all marched back to the same pile we had created the previous evening - and ordered to bag it all up again and take it to another boiler house. That was the pattern. Believe it or not, for ten days we shifted the same pile of coke around Chatham, often to the same space we had emptied it from a couple of days before. It seemed a bit pointless even then, but we were getting closer and closer to 'the day' and that was the important thing anyway.

Now, Dagenham is within easy reach of Chatham by train (at least it was when we had a proper train service) so I did have the opportunity to nip home for the weekend. With the double celebration of my 21st birthday and demob coming up as well, I was rather looking forward to my last weekend. Well I was until I found out that, on my birthday and my last Sunday as a sailor, I was rostered for guard duty. No one would swap duties with me so I resigned myself to having a few birthday bevvies in the NAAFI, before going on that guard duty watch on that Sunday night.

In fact, by the time we were due to go on watch at 10pm we had swallowed a fair amount of celebratory ale. We were not stoned out of our brains, but it would be fair to say we were 'gibbering' a little as we put on the official guard-duty belt and gaiters before lining up to be issued with our (unloaded) rifles.

There was no real security problem in those days - it was years before the IRA got serious. The Officer of the Watch went off to enjoy his bottle of wardroom gin, leaving the Leading Seaman in charge of the guard that night to organise us. One man on watch at a time - the rest could kip on the bare mattresses in an empty barrack room handily close by. We drew lots for an hour apiece - I drew the 1am to 2am slot and we all turned in, each of us having made a note of where the guy we had to wake up was sleeping.

I was duly shaken awake at five to one, and started my lonely vigil. All we had to do was take a turn or two around the parade ground. There was none of this nonsense about actually guarding the gate or anything. It was very quiet in the early hours and nothing stirred but, bearing in mind the amount of birthday booze I had sunk a few hours before, I was not at my brightest. After a turn or two around the parade ground I had to sit down and have a smoke, on one of the benches around it. God, I was tired!

Next thing I know, I am getting jabbed ferociously in the shoulder. Through my befuddled consciousness I could hear shouting, some of it appearing to question the legitimacy of my parentage. Blearily I became aware that the hollering was coming from a Lieutenant Commander who was also poking me with my own rifle to emphasise his point. What was worse was that behind him lurked a smirking female of the civilian variety who was clearly enjoying her bloke's macho performance.

Thankfully this guy was not the Officer of the Watch - he was probably back from a heavy night in Chatham, bringing the girl friend back to show her his itchings. So he never had the list of overnight sentries with names, but he was going potty anyway. Shrieking threats about Captain's Reports, he was demanding to know my name and number.

It was at this point that Engineer Mechanic Harrison rode to the rescue in my imagination.

I staggered to my feet and hauled myself up to attention, saluted and glibly reeled off his name and equally fictitious number - details that he even wrote down. Then he read me my fortune, thrust my rifle back at me and ordered me to report to the Master at Arms by noon. Then he swayed off, with giggling girl friend clinging to his arm, towards the officer's quarters and presumably a night of lust. I didn't have the heart to tell him I was actually planning to be in Dagenham by noon.

But then I realised I had another little problem. I looked at my watch, and saw it was 4.20am. I had not only done two other people's watches, I didn't know who to wake for the 4am slot, though I did know a mate who was on the 5am start. I had to stay on guard, making sure I stayed awake this time of course, until then.

The only way I managed that was by making sure I was walking, and walking, and walking all around that bloody parade ground in the early hours of that morning. Well, I had plenty to think about anyway, given that I had not only been caught sleeping on watch, I had lied to my back teeth about who I was as well. Eventually I staggered back to the dormitory and located the 5am man. I woke him and just fell onto my own bunk again

Only a couple of hours later we were noisily woken, lined up for inspection and dismissed. No one questioned why they had slept through their watch, and not a word about reports was said by the Officer of the Watch. So far, so good.

We were due to leave the place by 10.30am, so for the next few hours I was sweating a little bit. The final touch of irony was when we went to collect our travel warrants and the Navy made its last despairing efforts to get us to stay.

'Have you thought about signing on'?

'Yes sir!'

'You have? And what do you think about it'?

'No chance!'

'Right', his friendly tone changed, *'Here's your travel warrant, good-bye!'*

We could hardly get out of his office quick enough - but I had my own reasons for getting out as well. All morning, right up to the time we were handed that warrant, and we were walking out of the barracks gate laden down with kitbags I was on edge. I kept getting this nasty feeling I was about to hear an announcement over the public address system, inviting Engineer Mechanic Harrison to report to the Master at Arms.

It never was, and I wasn't going to hang about waiting for it, but I often wondered if an announcement was ever made for Engineer Mechanic Harrison C/K...whatever his number was.

Back in Civvy Street, my national duty done, I was a bit of a loss what to do. I still had cravings for a career at sea, though not with the Royal Navy, but could see no practical way of achieving it. So I went back to the Globe Pneumatic while I was thinking things over. It didn't take long (George White the foreman didn't exactly welcome me with open arms either) and within weeks I really was on my way back to sea again.

There was once a barmaid called Nell!

Within a few weeks of leaving Engineer Mechanic Lynch C/K946568 (and Harrison) behind me in Chatham Barracks, Merchant Navy Uncertificated Junior Engineer Officer Lynch was chugging across the Pacific. Having convinced a City shipping company that I was too good an opportunity to pass up (reminiscence 64), I was living it up in the good ship SS Southern Prince thanks to the Furness Withy Shipping Co.

For the company, the object of the voyage was to drop off a cargo of whisky, iron and cars in New Zealand, and then pop over to Australia for a few thousand bales of wool. In the event Oz managed without us, and we sailed round the coast of the Kiwis picking up the wool from its ports instead. As it happened these bales of wool caused me quite a problem before we got them home because, thanks to our holds being crammed to the top with the stuff, I actually had a bad bout of hay fever, which, considering we were smack in the middle of the Pacific, was a bit unexpected.

Having fled the Navy in December, I'd gone back to work in the Globe Pneumatic Engineering Company. This was not a proposition that met with anything but reluctance on the Globe's part because to be frank, I had not been one of the greatest of their apprentices in the first place. But, because I had been there before being wrenched from house and home to serve my country, they had to employ me anyway.

I didn't like it then, any more than I had a couple of years earlier. Although I was working for them as a lathe turner, earning quite good cash as it happens, I was looking for a way out before the end of my first tea break. It came when another of the former apprentices mentioned that he had done a trip with the Merchant Navy while I had been away. He enthused another one of the lads - Dennis Tibbett - as well as me, and before you could say 'can I have a day off please, guvnor' Dennis and I were in London's Leadenhall Street.

To cut a long story short, we were very soon in and booked for a berth in the Southern Prince as officers, ready to live the life of Riley being waited on hand and foot by stewards and with ready access to prolific amounts of booze.

That January Dennis and I joined the ship in Hull, just before she sailed to Ostend on a quick visit before coming back to the UK and up the Thames to the Victoria Docks. Apart from the personal reminder in the Channel that my stomach and I did not always agree on our enthusiasm on the sea, all was well so far. A few days in London - swaggering about at home yapping on about the ship - and we were off to Liverpool to spend three weeks refitting, and taking on our cargo.

I must admit I did like Liverpool. We had some great times ashore in the local pubs there and your average scouser really does have a great sense of humour. Thinking about it, I was in Liverpool in 1956 when young Paul, John and the others were probably playing church socials round the corner doing their Quarrymen bit.

The Southern Prince eventually sailed out into the Mersey straight into one of the worst storms the Irish Sea had seen in years. For the next five days and nights, as we headed out into the Atlantic, I was back to my old bucket-carrying engine room routines. It was a pretty bad experience I would prefer not to dwell on, but I do remember one grisly night, coming off watch and taking a glass of Andrews Liver Salts in the hope it would calm me down a bit. It was still fizzing as it came back again.

Then one day, my stomach stopped rocking round the clock and began to calm down a little. At last I began to enjoy the voyage as we left the wintry north Atlantic further and further behind us and headed towards the Caribbean, Panama and the canal.

First we had to bunker (take on oil) in Curacao at one of the huge oil terminals there. I remember a bright and sunny day, seeing another ship - a gleaming white passenger job - doing the same thing on the other side of the terminal. Now this oil is not your average diesel oil - it is thick black gungy stuff, which has to be heated and treated before it can actually be used in the boilers and engines.

Suddenly one of the oil pump lines on the smart white liner passenger snapped and began acting like a berserk hosepipe. Within seconds that gleaming white vessel was dripping black as the oil line sprayed it liberally with the oil it should have been pumping into its fuel tanks. Oh dear me, did we have a good old laugh from the decks of the Southern Prince?

I will never forget my first experience, a day or so later, of the Panama Canal. Ships are pulled through parts of it by 'mechanical donkeys' and we sat there on deck supping large gin and tonics, and eating crayfish salads as we watched the huge machines do our work. Then we motored gently under our own power through the jungle parts of the canal. I really did see crocodiles crawling down the bank into the water and heard the brightly coloured birds sitting on the branches as we passed through. It was hot and steamy day, and the freezing cold of Dagenham in January - not to mention the miserable atmosphere of the Globe Pneumatic - seemed a long way away.

We spent about five or six weeks in the Pacific on our way to New Zealand, usually without another ship in sight - though occasionally at night a brightly lit passenger ship would pass by on the horizon. At night we sailed, drinking ice-cold cans of beer, beneath a cloudless black ceiling containing unfamiliar stars. Peering over the side we could see the phosphorescence in the water and the flying fish skidding along the surface – sometimes even being bounced up onto our decks to flap helplessly unless someone picked them up to toss them over the side again.

It was a marvellous time. There I was, recent ragamuffin from the streets, and even more recently, a Royal Navy 'stoker' polishing brass and shifting piles of coke. Now I was a 'ship's officer', giving orders to 'stokers' and 'donkey greasers' down below on watch, while picking their brains and spending our time off watch swigging duty free gin, whisky and crates of cold beer. We not only crossed the equator, without ceremony, but the International Date Line too. (We had two Wednesdays one week on the outward trip and on the way back we had a week without one)

Then one day we arrived in New Zealand. I loved NZ. As the Prince cruised gently up the bay into an Auckland bathed in the warm sunlight of a February morning, we caught glimpses of this new (to some of us) and exciting world beyond the dock gates. We would be cruising around the North and South islands of this land of the Maoris for the next few months, and life was looking real sweet.

Even as we tied up and closed the engine room down dockies, as they always did wherever we were, swarmed aboard keen to do some private business before the local Customs arrived to spoil everything. They were brash, loud and loaded with NZ quids - and that was when the penny dropped with us younger seadogs. We hadn't been able to buy any duty free booze on board for a fortnight - clearly the more experienced Chief Mate and Second Engineer had stocked up in advance. They did some good business that morning.

To us, New Zealand was amazing in those days. In the weeks we were there we swam off its beaches, chatted up some pretty gorgeous Kiwi-birds (unfeathered sort), fished with the local kids for barracuda off our decks, and set out to hitch-hike to the famous hot springs of Rotarua. I failed miserably in that venture because of the difficulties experienced in getting past the pub at the end of the jetty, but years later my son went to that country and brought me back a tablet of Rotarua Mud Soap. Then there was the famous 'Five'o-clock Swill'.

Things have changed a great deal now and in both NZ

and Oz they keep more civilised drinking hours these days. Back then, the pubs shut at 6pm on the dot - just sixty minutes after the normal working day ended at 5pm. Clearly that did not leave a great deal of time for after-work jollies for the drinking classes down under.

We were ok - we kept ship's hours not dockies hours. It had been a thirsty trip however (especially during the last two weeks) so when Fourth Engineer Duncan McMasters, who'd already done one trip on the ship, suggested we popped out for a beer or three in the nearest pub about four o'clock on that first day, we were easily swayed.

This pub was in clear view, about two hundred yards from the dock gates and was, by any English pub standards, fairly basic. Not exactly the 'spit and sawdust' jobs we were used to outside British dock gates, but well scrubbed tables and solid wooden chairs - no carpet, a long highly polished bar totally uncluttered by the usual sort of bar furniture, like ashtrays, beer mats or bar towels. Standing behind this bar there was a barmaid called, I swear to God, Nell.

When four boiler-suited Limeys walked in, Nell was already standing ready with a long half-inch rubber tube in hand. In front of her, the bar was covered with small half-pint sized glasses - dozens of them. We ordered four beers and she used the tube, which had a kind of clamp on it, to squirt beer into four glasses for us, charging us sixpence a glass.

It seemed a bit odd because we were the only ones in the pub yet all these glasses were laid out like it was party time in a Portsmouth NAAFI before a big ship sailed. McMasters, having been there before, smiled knowingly and indicated to us to sit down.

The clocked ticked on and we bought a few more beers. It wasn't the greatest beer on earth - to be honest it was lousy and tasted more of acorns than hops. We knew that after 6 o'clock we would have to go back to the ship to find a decent drink anyway, so by quarter to five we'd already had a few tanners worth of the acorn stuff. Nell, by then, was clearly getting ready for something because she had started to squirt beer into glasses that no one had ordered.

Suddenly we became aware that out of the window a few hundred yards away something was happening. The dock gates were wide open, but although there was clearly a crowd there, no one was coming out of them though we could see them all glancing at their watches. McMasters hurriedly got a double round in for us and at 5pm a siren, apparently signalling the end of the day's work, blared out. What followed has remained with me ever since.

It was like the start of a frenzied London Marathon - but these runners were not all on foot. Some of them made a dash for it on bikes and motor bikes - even a car or two was roaring through those dock gates before the siren had even come to the end of its wailing.

The shrewder boozers had positioned themselves in the right strategic spot, not so much for a quick getaway, but to make sure that when they reached the finish line they were in front of a convenient door. Their destination was our pub, and we sat there open-mouthed watching through the window as this torrent of human thirst - a tsunami of desperate dockies. - came rushing towards us.

They were running and leaping, jumping and swerving in and out on their bikes and motorbikes - how nobody got mown down in the crush I will never know. As the first notes of the siren reached our ears Nell had upped her speed, and was squirting away like a galvanised stirrup pump. Within seconds the pub doors had burst open, and the 'Swill' was under way.

Sixpenny pieces rained down onto the bar in a silver shower as eager hands grabbed and spilled beer everywhere. What had been a quiet and almost empty pub was suddenly packed and heaving, as dockies forced their way to the front shouting, cussing, yelling and demanding. In front of if all stood Nell, calm and impassive in the pandemonium, scooping up tanners and squirting that lousy beer into empty glasses, filling, refilling and rerefilling them as fast as it was disappearing down throats.

These lads had just one hour's drinking time a day - and clearly it wasn't ever wasted in small talk. This was the famous Five o'clock Swill at its cutting, or rather drinking, edge. This was serious boozing. We 'hard drinking' young Brits learned a lot that day - like make sure that in future we had an hour's worth of beer in front of us before the clock struck 5.

I have seen some drinking in my day - have even occasionally been party to some of it - but I have never before, or since, seen anything like the Swill. An hour later these blokes were falling all over the place, happily stoned out of their brains on that acorn brew as Nell threw them out so she could close up.

As Winston Churchill, himself something of a toper and bit of an authority on Finest Hours, might have said: "Never before, in the field of human dehydration, was so much downed so fast, by so many".

Yes, I was a fellow traveller!
I was never a Russian spy - but somewhere in the files of the FBI in Washington there is still a file, fingerprints and a big question mark against my name - because I drank my way across the Atlantic with a Russian diplomat.

I met Nikolai Kalin on a transatlantic liner - the Ile de France - back in the late fifties. Furness Withy was sending me to New York to join a small tramp steamer called the Fort Avalon (what an experience that turned out to be), and had booked me a steerage cabin in the Ile de France to get there. (If I had been travelling with crew, as an officer I would have been booked into a second-class cabin).

When I'd walked into Furness Withy after coming back from New Zealand I told them I was ready to go back to sea but fancied a steam driven, rather than diesel motor, ship this time. As it happened they did have such a ship and asked if I could leave the next day for New York on the Queen Mary. Sadly I had to point out I had no passport or American visa, so they told me to go away and get them and be ready to be shipped out the following week on a different transatlantic liner.

The ship I was to join was a steam turbine job called the Fort Avalon and she was trading out of New York, sailing up and down America and Canada's Eastern seaboard of the states to Main, Newfoundland, Nova Scotia and occasionally down to Bermuda. First though I had to get to the Big Apple and they booked me onto the Ile de France.

This was not a crossing I looked forward to with any great enthusiasm and even less so once we had all clambered aboard in Southampton from the tender that took us out to where the liner was moored. The other three passengers in my cabin were young Yank students going home to Mom and Pop. The worst thing was that some iffy experiences in France, when I was serving in the RN a few years earlier, had not exactly left me with a feeling of great affection towards the French either.

As things turned out, I had one major advantage – a British Merchant Navy officer's uniform. This actually consisted of a navy blue battledress with a couple of gold epaulettes, dark blue trousers and a cap which had been issued to my busman father some years previously, but which now bore a Merchant Navy cap-badge. This bundle of hand-me-downs proved to be a passport to alcoholic oblivion. It didn't matter that I had been at sea for only a few years - and two of them as a Royal Navy 'stoker', working in noisy MTB engine rooms so I never actually mentioned it.

The appearance of a young English speaking naval officer - albeit a British merchant naval officer - worked miracles. Suitably clad, whenever I wandered into a bar in that ship fellow passengers would make a beeline for me for a chat. They were keen to get my views on the kind of trip we were having, and how the Ile de France compared with the Queen Mary (a view I was more than delighted to express despite never actually having seen, let alone sailed in, either of the great Cunard ships).

I only ever spent my own cash on my first drink. From then on I was entertained very royally by dollar-rich Americans going home after their vacation in a Europe still rebuilding after the war. There were also some European businessmen travelling to explore the New World opportunities and pick my brains on the best places to eat in New York. (I'd only ever heard of one, so spent a lot of time recommending Jack Dempsey's Restaurant) Then there was Nikolai, a man who was also very clearly flush with dosh and keen to drink most of it.

We met on the first night out. You couldn't help but notice the guy really because he was a giant of a man. He stood well over six foot, had shoulders like the proverbial barn door and spoke better English than I did. He was also clearly in need of company because although his wife and family were aboard, he spent every evening drinking in the bar without them. In fact the only time I only ever saw them was when they all disembarked in New York a week later.

Nikolai and I were close buddies within an hour or so on the first night out from Southampton, almost before we were out of the Solent in fact; but it took a few drinks before he admitted he was Russian. He'd fought in Stalingrad, of course, as a very young boy (didn't they all?), so I told him some dramatic tales about my dad who had seen action during the Battle of Britain, as one of the Few.

Well, yes he was 'flying' trolley buses rather than Spitfires and Hurricanes, but they were often few and far between, and I wasn't going to let Kalin have it all his own way. Anyway we'd all seen action in the Battle of Britain - watching the RAF slugging it out with the Luftwaffe from the ground, and collecting the shrapnel from the garden the next day.

Nik and I actually got quite close during that week as we crossed the Atlantic. Cheerfully, lips loosened with the help of the alcohol, we debated the Cold War, the price of cabbages in Moscow, and I was able to dispel the rumour that British families only had one pair of shoes between them.

We also touched on the different reasons for our journey. It turned out he was a diplomat on his way to join the Russian delegation in the United Nations. I told him how I would be in a cargo ship cruising up and down the American East coast - he seemed quite interested in that. He also enjoyed hearing about my experiences serving in the Royal Navy's MTBs a few years earlier. We pledged to meet up in New York to renew our friendship once we got settled. Well, you do, right?

He was a real nice guy actually and made a trip that held all the promise of a wet weekend in Bognor into a bit of a pleasure cruise. Even better, he flashed a big wad of Kruschev's roubles and we did our best to start a run on the Central Bank of Moscow by emptying the Ile de France's beer cellar on a nightly basis. Of course, it all had to end sooner or later. On the sixth morning I had my first bleary-eyed sight of the Statue of Liberty, as the famous skyline of New York loomed out of the early morning mist. Within the hour we were docked in the great transatlantic liner terminals near Manhattan.

My instructions were to stay on board and wait to be contacted by the shipping agent. I was leaning over a rail, actually waving a cheerful goodbye to Nikolai and his family who were being hustled through the immigration area, when a little guy wearing a snazzy suit and Brooklyn accent suddenly appeared on my shoulder and introduced himself.

Checking that I was who he'd thought I was he said I had to go and see the doctor at immigration but he'd pulled a few strings to get us quick access. He grabbed one of my cases and we went ashore to a big dockside shed, where I was introduced to 'the doctor'. This guy held out his hand for my Seaman's Discharge Book, and my passport with its visa to the United States of America, scanning them thoroughly before glaring up at me.

"Whadya here for?" He seemed a touch unfriendly. My shipping agent escort started to explain and he turned on him, almost snarling at him to be quiet. "Can't da guy speak for himself?" he snapped.

I mumbled that I was there to join the Fort Avalon, which was a British cargo ship trading out of New York. Then he started firing all sorts of questions at me, and none of them health related or concerned about my well-being.

"You ever been a Communist, a fellow traveller or member of any organisation connected to the Communist Party"?

I assured him that, apart from once being a member of the Associated Engineering Union, I had not. I pointed pit that in fact I'd signed a declaration to that effect before they would even give me a visa. His questions got odder - and still none of them of them medically related or asking about my health, but the unnerving thing was that he was writing it all down on a big form. Then he started to ask me about the actual voyage, and who I'd met on the Ile de France and suddenly the penny dropped.

I had not been watched specifically - but Kalin had clearly been under surveillance, probably from the moment he left Russia so anyone he was with had been noted down for the FBI. I guess Kalin knew that anyway because being watched is par for the course when it comes to diplomats, and especially so in the Cold War days.

In fact FBI knew more about what I'd been doing on that voyage than I did - mainly because I'd been boozed during most of it - and he quizzed me for what seemed like an hour, obviously convinced that the KGB had recruited me. Finally, somewhat grudgingly, he stamped my entry permit and opened America to me without actually saying welcome.

I was sailing in and out of New York for a year after that, but never saw Kalin again. It was at a time when America was incredibly paranoid about the Russians. I remember one day the Avalon docked in Brooklyn just as the news broke about the Russians sending the first Sputnik satellite into space.

That happened on October 4th 1957, and the news broke on every radio station just as we came upriver to Brooklyn. At first we dismissed the media excitement as just that - but when we docked and the longshoremen came aboard, it was all they were talking about. As was our usual routine, for us it was a quick shower, change and off into Manhattan in a Yellow Cab. That was where we got the full blast from a clearly concerned cabbie.

"Didja see what dose Goddammed Russkis have dun? Dat Goddammed ting is up there right now, looking down on us. Goddammed Commies..." That was the general tone, albeit in pukka Brooklynese rather than my version, of the entire journey into the city. Frankly the guy was in a blind panic - and astonishingly it seemed the entire city was as well.

You have to remember this took the Americans, well all of us, completely by surprise. The Americans had been working on putting a rocket into space since the end of the war when a bunch of ex-Nazi rocketeers like Werner Von Braun had fallen into their hands, while Stalin picked up some himself. What the Russians had proved was that their Germans had been shown to be better than the Yank's Germans had been.

Of course, it would be an exaggeration to claim that they were putting up armoured shutters and digging deep shelters, but there is no doubt that as far as New York was concerned that day, the news was grave indeed. Hotel doormen, interviewed on TV, were sagely observing that there were no military uniforms on the streets of the city - which presumably led them the conclusion that all military leave had been cancelled with men ordered back to barracks.

Other rumours swept the city. Bartenders, always good for a rumour or three, had it on good authority that Russian submarines had been spotted in the Hudson River, and later our own radio officer told us about a barber he had gone to for a trim in Brooklyn who'd actually had a pistol stuck in his belt to deal with any red parachutists that floated past his door.

It took a great deal of Washington reassurance to calm things down and then, just as they had - the bloody Russkis sent another satellite into orbit, this one containing a dog called Laika.

By that time the Fort Avalon was cruising up and down Newfoundland, so whether or not the barmen were seeing submarines again or not never really mattered to us. Anyway I had Russian friends.

The Fort Avalon
I have never written a great deal about the Fort Avalon before yet I don't really know why, because I have always felt it to be the finest year of my young life. Years later I even

harboured the idea of going back to her, but it turned out she'd been long sold and renamed.

This was a love affair that began one fine day in 1957, when a New York yellow cab deposited my new Chief Engineer (I seem to remember his name was Jordan) and me, onto the dockside at Bush Terminal in Brooklyn, where she'd tied up only half an hour earlier. Jordan and I had been put up in the Times Square Hotel for a few days, after I'd left the Il de France where I'd been a passenger crossing the Atlantic, because the Avalon been late coming in. I'd had a great couple of days rubbernecking in the Big Apple living it up on a few dollars a day expenses, eating out in some great restaurants and meeting Jordan for the first time.

First impressions of a ship are always sketchy, because although this one was only 3.500 tons, as against the 8000-ton Southern Prince, from the jetty she looked just as huge. We struggled with our gear up the gangway onto the deck where we were met by the Chief Engineer who was leaving and who took Jordan off to his office.

The Second Engineer was a Geordie called Bill Thomas and he took charge of me, showed me into the 'Engineers Alley' where he introduced me to the Third, Fourth and Fifth engineers - another Geordie, a Scot and a Hampshire man. I was to be the Junior Engineer for one trip, after which I would be the Fifth Engineer replacing the on who would be leaving the ship when it got back to New York in three weeks. (When he did we were joined by a Scouser who took over my job, so the UK ports were pretty well represented).

The Fort Avalon was a trader that also occasionally carried a couple of passengers. Its usual trip, after leaving New York, was to St John (Maine) then Halifax (Nova Scotia) before going on to St John's in Newfoundland to unload the rest of whatever cargo we carried. Then we'd go to another Newfoundland port called Corner Brook where the great lumber mills had turned trees into newsprint – great rolls of which was carried back to New York.

Occasionally the route varied – two or three times we went down to Bermuda and once to a 'one horse' town called Port Union in Newfoundland. There we successfully managed to pull down a brand newly build wooden jetty because someone was slow in cutting the forward lines as we steamed away.

A steamship she was driven by a turbine engine, powered by steam produced in a couple of big oil fed boilers. That was our domain of course, but I will never forget the first words spoken to me by my new shipmates, that first morning in Bush Terminal. *'Do you drink?'*

I assured them that I had been known to quaff the odd beer or three and they tossed over a large holdall. Having just closed down the engine room they were still wearing overalls of course but they told me there was no beer left in the ship. They threw some money together between them and asked me to go down to the end of the jetty, where there was a 'dockies' canteen, and fill the bag up.

I was young, fit and fairly strong but by the time the bag had been filled with enough bottles of Budweiser to cope with the money I'd brought, I could hardly lift it. But I managed it and by the time I got back aboard they were cleaned up and ready for a drink and proper introductions. Within the hour I was smashed out of my brain and we were all best buddies.

So much so that I agreed to go ashore into Manhattan with them to visit the Merchant Navy Officers Club, where more booze passed our lips and by which time we'd all become real shipmates.

A yellow cab back to Bush Terminal which we reached to find that the Fort Avalon was being moved along the dock a hundred yards, so we had to wait a few minutes before we could get back aboard. By the time the gangway was in place I was totally legless and my new skipper, Captain Robert Baxter-Powell watched from the bridge as his newest officer was carried feet first back on board.

At breakfast in the officers saloon the next morning I was formally introduced to B-P, who made it quite clear that he expected standards from his officers, even engineering officers, higher than he'd witnessed the previous night.

It was time to get down to some serious work though and, although a lot of shore based maintenance work was going on around us, I was introduced to my duties. I would be working the 4-8 watches (4am-8am, 4pm-8pm) with Bill Thomas, the Second Engineer, mostly doing routine work that also included testing the boiler water every day for its alkaline and acid levels. The engine itself was a huge (to me) steam turbine job, which I would eventually be shown how to drive, though my first job when preparing for sea was to go aft and check the steering gear.

A couple of days later we were cargoed up and ready for sea – I was quite happy and looking forward to it all, but there was a problem. The seamen on board (mainly Newfoundlanders) had gone on strike. It took hours before all that was settled and we headed out of the Hudson en route to the Atlantic and Maine, where St John was our first and usual port of call.

One happy result was that for some reason the Fort Avalon was the first, and only, ship I was never seasick on, but by God she was a hard drinking ship and it turned out that that first day had been just about par for the course. Apart from Bill Thomas I cannot remember all their names now, but they were the best bunch of men I ever sailed with and all believed passionately in the 'work hard play hard' way of life. The engineer's alleyway always had a party going on, with bottles of gin or boxes (24) of Budweisers flowing freely

We went to Bermuda a couple of times and after we left

on one trip we all celebrated in Bill Thomas' cabin with 90pcnt proof Bermuda rum. Great, until 4am when it was time to get up for the watch – I made it down there alright, but Bill didn't appear.

Throughout the watch that morning I kept sending a stoker up to shake him but he couldn't be shaken and I was doing the job I wasn't technically qualified to do. I even 'blew the funnels' – an exercise which involved blasting all the soot out of the funnels to clean them, and for which the ship had to alter course so she was sailing into the wind. I did all that without the bridge realising they had a complete amateur in the engine room, and it wasn't until 7.15 that we finally managed to wake the Second engineer.

We sailed the Avalon through all kinds of weather – a back end of a hurricane when the entire stern was being lifted out of the water. We had to quickly shut the steam down until she settled back down again. If we'd left the steam on the screw (propeller) would have spun so fast it could have come apart – so it was quite a dangerous time. On other occasions, off the coast of Newfoundland during the winter, big chunks of pack ice would thud into the side of the ship giving you the nasty feeling that we were about to have a Titanic moment.

Perhaps one of the worst things that did happen was when we had an engine failure one day, and it was a case of all hands down into the engine room. The ship lost power of course and was drifting towards the coast so much there was even talk of calling the local coastguard out for help. We kept getting phone calls in the engine room asking for progress, and Jordan kept shouting back at them to give us a chance.

Finally, we sorted the problem and reported to the bridge that we could get under way again. There was an immediate demand for reverse engine followed by another ring on the telegraph to resume normal speeds. I went up on deck for a breather and almost collapsed – we had been yards from some of the most vicious rocks outside Cornwall. Baxter-Powell, presumably keen to ensure there was no salvage issue involved, had taken a gamble on our getting the ship going again.

I loved New York, and its people, but I suppose the place that made the biggest impression on me was Bermuda and the Caribbean. We visited Hamilton, its top town, twice and apart from going through the Panama Canal in the Southern Prince, this was the nearest I had been to the West Indies.

The pink sands, clean air and wonderful climate, the old town where I bought my first Brownie cine-camera. We'd hire small motorbikes, mopeds really, and ride up into the hinterland of the island to visit a pub called the Smugglers Inn, where we drank their famous 'swizzles', which resulted in a few dizzy moments actually riding the bikes back to Hamilton. We would also buy the 90pcnt-proof rum that mixed so well with the coca cola that was responsible for our being unable to get the second engineer down on his watch that memorable morning.

It was in Bermuda that we tied up alongside one of Furness Withy's other ships – the Queen of Bermuda, which had just lost one of its stewards, Tommy Hicks. His stage name was Tommy Steele and by then he was making it big back home as our first real rock and roller.

Thanks largely to Bermuda it was a year I remember the Fort Avalon for, but it all went sour not long after our second visit there - which was also when we ran into the back end of a hurricane in the 'Triangle' that could have caused us so many problems. Whether it was the strain of that experience, or other personal problems he had, I don't know but on the way back to New York our chief engineer (Jordan, who I'd joined the ship with) had a bit of a nervous breakdown. When we got back to the Big Apple he had to be taken off the ship.

For one trip Bill Thomas, our second, was made up to chief engineer and we all got moved up a slot. In my case that meant being the fourth engineer for while, handling my own watch (8-12) and being in charge of the refrigeration unit. I knew next to nothing about refrigeration, but it did mean that I had a key to the cold room and as a result we had some great lobster sandwiches in the engineer's alley that trip. That upset Baxter Powell because they were his personal stock of Maine lobsters and he actually held an enquiry to establish why some were missing.

I was the first under suspicion of course (I had the key), but I acted so indignantly over the allegation that he hurriedly apologised to me and said it was probably down to the ship's cook.

When we got back to New York a new man, 'Dickie' Bird, arrived to take up the job of Chief Engineer. He knew the ship fairly well, having sailed on her before, and he had a bit of a nasty reputation. It took him just over an hour to get on the wrong side of us when he tried to block our booze. Even worse he upset our stokers too and I am sure that at one stage on that next trip one of them tried to do him some serious damage because a particularly heavy spanner fell through the floor grating to miss his head by an inch.

By the time we got back to New York we had all had enough and to a man demanded to end our articles – refusing to sail with him on board. It caused a bit of a ruckus with executives even being flown out from London to find out what was happening and why they had an officer's mutiny on their hands. One by one we were all interviewed and made our cases against Bird – arguments which appeared to be accepted and he did apologise, so we all agreed to sail again for one more trip, half expecting to stay on for the remainder of our articles.

When we got back to New York though a new set of engineers was waiting to take over from us, and we were paid off and sent home. We travelled back on the SS United States, which at the time held the Blue Riband for quick crossings of the Atlantic, happy and unaware that as far as Furness Withy as concerned, our cards were marked.

It was eighteen months before I could get another ship, and that was about the worst and most dangerous vessel – the SS Superiority – I ever sailed in. That trip lasted a month in the Baltic before coming home and I paid off in Glasgow. It was the last ship I ever signed articles on, but it will always be the Fort Avalon that I remember with affection.

It was a great time to be the age I was, in New York and on the North Atlantic. In fact, if I have to point to any particular year in my life it would be 1957/58, on that beaten up old tramp steamer that gave me so much in terms of pleasure and experience. Not simply because it was a 'hard drinking – hard playing' ship but, while over many years I have experienced great comradeship – I have never, before or since, felt camaraderie as deep and sincere as that we had on the Fort Avalon.

And talking of the Superiority…

Yes, I paid the ferryman

I had been warned. The guy in the Ship's Officers Pool emphasised that in no way would he offer one of Everard's ships to any young Merchant Navy officer; but I was young, unattached and itching to get back to sea again.

The fact that there was quite a serious shipping slump on at the time is probably why I should have known better. The speed with which I was accepted - a telegram following an initial tentative enquiry by letter - in the late 50s, should have had the warning bells going like the clappers. All I could see, though, was the telegram appointing me 4th Engineer on the SS Superiority and urging me to report to Greenhithe (on the south bank of the Thames) with all speed.

I hurriedly gave a week's notice to King George's Hospital where I'd been working as a maintenance engineer and packed my kit. Dad drove me across the Thames to the company's offices where I had understood I would be joining my new ship. I was greeted with open arms and invited to stow my gear on board an old ship that happened to be tied up on the jetty, but was very clearly not the Superiority.

Now I had emphasised in my letter that in no way did I want to join an oil tanker - which this near derelict wreck very clearly was (or at least had been in its day). I was assured that this was just a transit holding berth until the Superiority docked. Fair enough - I lugged my cases aboard and waited…and waited.

By 4 o'clock I was getting a bit worried. I had spent a lunch hour (or two) in a dockside pub with other in-transit chaps, but clearly the quicker I was aboard my new ship the better. Problem was there was very little sign of any more boats coming up the Thames that day. At 4.30pm I knocked at the shipping office door again and asked what was happening.

Oh dear! Oh dear! They had forgotten completely about me. Yes the Superiority had docked… in Methil, near Kirkaldy on the Firth of Forth, and *'Oh yes, here is your train ticket for the overnight train to Scotland.'*

Now this was a very disturbing development. Again I recalled the smirk on the face of that Officer's Pool bloke who'd warned me about this particular company. Still as I have said I was young, unattached and totally bloody stupid, so off I dashed to London laden down with my gear to catch the train to Scotland.

There were only two of us in the compartment that night as we rattled towards the Land of the Rising Haggis, and as it happened he was also a merchant seaman, on his way home to Newcastle after signing off a ship in the Albert Dock. We kept each other company, happily chatting and drinking his duty free Scotch as we chugged north through the night. By the time he got off on Tyneside I was having a bit of a job keeping my eyes open, but I had to change at Edinburgh so I forced myself to stay awake.

It was a pretty grim, cold and misty, February morning when I got off the local train from Edinburgh onto Kirkaldy station. Both Kirkaldy and I were, to put it mildly, tired and dirty so it didn't help matters much to find no taxis at the station. I was directed to go to the nearest bus stop where I could get a morning workers bus to Methil Docks.

Docks are easy to find. All you need do is look for masts and cranes, and keep an ear out for the seagulls, so actually finding them once I'd been decamped from the bus outside the gates wasn't a problem. I staggered along the dockside, weighed down with cases, holdalls and my portable Dansette (record player), looking for my new ship. Suddenly I came to a part of the dockside that sort of stopped. It restarted some thirty or so yards further on, but that narrow gap had a few million gallons of the Firth of Forth flowing through it, and there seemed to be a marked lack of bridges in the neighbourhood.

A somewhat scruffy looking individual was standing nearby. Since he wore a thick roll neck jersey and peaked cap, I guessed he might be a good bet to ask if the Superiority was in port and, if so, where the hell was she.

He thought for a moment, and then pointed vaguely through the mist, across that watery void, and telling me in thick Anglo-Gaelic, that there was a ship on the other dock over there that might well be the one I was looking for. Great, but how do I reach it? He revealed I was lucky because he was 'the ferryman', and all I needed to do was get my gear into his boat and he would row me across the gap to the other side.

Easy, huh? Well, yes - but I am here to tell you that this was no Woolwich Free Ferry. First you had to climb down an iron-rung ladder that was fixed to the wall of the dock into his rowing boat. Then you had to stand in it as he lowered your luggage down to you on the end of a rope. That done, he joined me in the boat, rowed the few yards across, stuck his hand out for a quid, and then tied my luggage back onto the rope for me to pull up once I had climbed another ladder onto the dockside. Nothing to it really - especially for a guy who had been awake for the best part of 24-hours, travelling the length of the land on a train and bottle of whisky.

Eventually, luggage stacked all around me, I stood on the other dockside as my ferryman rowed back. I found myself staring, with growing unease turning to horror, at the shape that was emerging out of the thinning mist. It was indeed the 3,500-ton SS Superiority - its once-smart yellow livery now liberally smeared with a thick coating of Polish coaldust. Even as I watched winches working on the hatches were hauling out tons of loose coal, some of it spilling out and dropping in great chunks onto the deck. More of that acrid black dust filled the air, and the ship, with a choking vapour as the cranes and winches poured coal into the dockside coal-trucks. I looked back - the ferryman had vanished back to the other side.

Without a shadow of any doubt the steamship Superiority was the filthiest and scruffiest dog of a vessel I had ever seen, let alone signed articles on. It was a floating slum and I was its 4th Engineer. I must have been stark, staring, and raving bloody mad.

In fact, after a month of sailing round the Baltic in mid-winter, on a ship with a freshwater tank on the upper deck which needed unfreezing every morning, a cabin awash with sea-water whenever the slightest sea was running and a cook whose skill and concept of hygiene would have done credit to an Albanian squat, I was quite enthusiastic about signing off her again.

During that four weeks we'd had armed guards on the gangway to stop us seeing Poland, suffered a second-to-none chucking-out routine in a Danish pub, seas so exuberant I lost my denture to the North Sea through a bilge-pipe, and cooking so bizarre I lived on bread and onion sandwiches for the entire trip.

'Carry on up the Baltic' never even came into it. That quid I spent on the ferryman was the worst money I ever spent, that's for sure. I hadn't been seasick for almost three years - mainly because a maintenance engineer in King George's Hospital in Ilford, never really had to contend with that many storm-tossed seas and Baltic blizzards.

I have been in ships that had rolled, in some that had pitched and tossed, while a few had even done submarine dips in the slightest swell. Until I joined the SS Superiority I had never before been in one capable of every waterborne acrobatic convulsion known to man. Whoever had designed that bloody ship must have passed his Naval Architect exams by correspondence course, while living it up in the funny farm.

OK, so the geyser might never have appreciated that his little floating masterpiece would become a Baltic trader, when he positioned the freshwater tank on the upper-deck with unlagged pipes. He might never have known that, within hours of leaving Scotland (in February) heading North, every toilet in that floating dustbin, apart from the engineer's one which was positioned above the main boiler, would be frozen solid -and we are talking frozen salt water here, not freshwater.

Even before we sailed, I'd realised I was in a spot of

bother, because I had met the ship's cook and had decided that a fairly strict 'bread and Spanish Onion' diet for the next three weeks might not be a bad idea. They were the only foodstuffs I knew he would have kept his hands off, because they came aboard before we sailed and didn't need his hands on them.

I had upset things from the start. As soon as I had staggered aboard and been introduced to the Chief Engineer, we'd fallen out because I insisted in getting some sleep before I went near a boiler suit. That did not go down too well but, after a bit of a barney he had grudgingly accepted it. Then, just before we sailed I'd been ordered, as the ship's fourth engineer, to the galley to fix a leaking diesel pipe on the stove so the ship's cook could get on with dinner.

There he sat - Albert Steptoe revisited. Sitting on a stool in the middle of the galley, he was peeling spuds and tossing them over his shoulder into a large saucepan, clearly meant for our dinner. Scruffy and unshaven, he was dressed in a stained tartan shirt and dark shiny trousers and wore a 'flat cap' that had clearly seen many a voyage; but the worst thing was that his aim was not too clever either. More often than not the peeled spud would leave his, somewhat grimy, hand and completely miss its target. They kept falling into a puddle of diesel oil caused by the very leak I had been sent to sort out.

Not to worry - the guy just picked the spud out of the puddle, rubbed it on the side of his shirt and threw it into the saucepan anyway. Eat your heart out Delia Smith, Ainsley Harrison et al. Well, it turns you right off your dinner and anything else he is likely to cook, right? I decided that I would exist on sandwiches, which I would make myself - and in the event they turned out to be onion sandwiches.

We left Methil, and the Firth of Forth, enroute for

Aalborg in Denmark. From there we were to sail to Stettin in Poland, still very much behind the Iron Curtain then of course. Then it was back to Aalborg before returning to Scotland - to Glasgow on the Clyde - a three or four week voyage, in the middle of winter through some of the coldest and wildest seas in the business and in a tub that had disaster written all over her. (A year later her sister ship went down in the Irish Sea with all hands during a storm).

I have already drawn attention to the fact that while I enjoyed the sea, my stomach did not and it wasn't long after leaving Scotland that I was back in my old routine of going down into the engine room armed with a bucket. Almost immediately I came to grief because, while I was cleaning out an oil filter, I vomited my front teeth denture, which disappeared before I could stop it, out of reach into a bilge pump - and thence, presumably, into the North Sea. We bounced all the way to the Baltic.

For me Denmark was forgettable from the start. As we arrived I was still below shutting down the engine room as the usual dockies came aboard, and I had forgotten the elementary rules about locking cabin doors while in port. So within ten minutes of being on Danish soil I was burgled, losing my wallet. Even worse they nicked a full bottle of duty-paid Scotch I had brought aboard and which I had not exactly been interested in during the turbulent voyage across the North Sea.

Then, just to really rub it in, I opened my wardrobe to check whether those thieving Danes had left me anything. There was my luggage - floating in about a foot of seawater. Wonderful - of all the cabins in that ship, I got the one that with a leaking wardrobe.

I'll come back to Denmark, but Poland - well now that was a real education. By the time we got there, having clunked our way through hundreds of miles of Baltic ice-fields of 'frozen solid waves', I had a regular morning chore - unfreezing the water tank pipes.

Every morning, before breakfast and in whatever seas happened to be running at the time I had to clamber up onto the upper deck in the freezing cold, wrap some paraffin-soaked rags around the pipes and set them alight. By the time we got to Stettin I was relieved that we were at least not heaving about all over the show as I was doing that. Yes, ok, we had a deep layer of snow all around us, but my innards could handle that.

That first morning I was up there wrapping my rags, and getting ready with the lighter, when I heard the unmistakable and still very familiar sound of – marching boots. I knew that noise only too well - it wasn't that long since I had been a 'marching boot' myself doing the biz on parade grounds. This lot though, seemed a lot more purposeful as I glanced up from my desktop 'bonfire'. It was a bunch of Polish squaddies, marching along the dockside towards us and they were armed to the teeth.

They halted, an officer bawled out something totally incomprehensible, and one of his lads stepped smartly forward, rifle at the ready, to take his place at the foot of our gangway. He was our guard, clearly there to protect us, or at least to make sure none of us slipped ashore to go spying for the CIA. To be honest none of us had any intention of doing any such thing, but I tell you he scared the life out of us.

That night a coach with darkened windows took the entire ships company ashore - to the dock canteen for the only entertainment available in that miserable place. Everyone, that is, except me. I drew the short straw in the engineer's alleyway, and had to remain on board as Officer of the Watch to run the generator and make sure the duty seaman adjusted the ropes holding us to the jetty as the tide changed.

I did feel a bit sorry for the guy on the gangway though, so when I made myself some hot chocolate and a bread and onion sandwich (I had maintained my diet), I made him some as well, offering it by using sign language of course. That poor sod had been on duty for hours, keeping himself warm by occasionally marching up and down and stamping his feet and believe me it was a touch chilly out there.

As I offered him the sandwich and mug he glanced furtively around to make sure we weren't being watched. Then he grabbed the sandwich and shoved it into the pocket of his greatcoat before holding out his hand for the steaming cup I was proffering. Taking it, another swift glance around, and he swallowed the lot in one big gulp.

I kid you not - that stuff was so hot I was still sipping mine, but he threw his mugfull down like he had an asbestos throat, clearly keen to do so before his guard commander came back and spotted him fraternising with me. He grinned his thanks as he handed me back the mug, and I watched as he went back on sentry duty - surreptitiously shoving his hand into his pocket and coming out with pieces of the onion sandwich, which he shoved into his mouth like it was his last supper.

When we got back to Aalborg, after leaving Stettin, I went ashore - with the third engineer for a beer or three. All we had to remember was that the Superiority was berthed in the 'Cement Fabrik' (cement factory) when it was time to come back aboard. Now you would think that was a simple thing, wouldn't you? Don't you believe it! It was Sunday and Aalborg was shut.

Drink we could buy - but proper grub other than the odd sandwich was definitely not on the cards. For me it was the defining moment - the last straw. Well almost.

We found ourselves a little bar in the middle of town and began some serious lager drinking. No food, just the drink and it went on for some hours but we had no real idea of just how late it was until the barman started stacking chairs. He was clearly sending a message, but it never stopped him serving us another two bottles of lager apiece.

Having done so, however, he then highlighted his previous message by opening the bloody door and letting the cool Baltic breezes blow in. OK, we picked up our bottles and wandered outside where, having carefully hidden our open bottles in our coat pockets he never saw the, we found a taxi.

'Cement Fabrik', we said - only to be met by a torrent of Danish. We had clearly met the only non-English-speaking Dane in town. He drove us to a police station where someone came out to interpret. The snow was coming down in blizzard proportions and we were getting steadily more careless with the open bottles in our pockets. It turned out there were seven 'cement fabriks' in Aalborg - all we had to find out was which one.

There was only one way - we had to do a very expensive conducted tour of the docks until finally, enveloped in darkness against the snow, we spotted the Superiority. My colleague jumped out of the cab - I jumped out...tripped and went headfirst into a six-foot snowdrift. The taxi-driver helped pull me out, and then discovered that our lager had been fizzing out of our pockets all over his back seat for the last leg of the tour. He was not best pleased - and nor were we when we got aboard to find all the power off and had to get our boiler suits back on again to solve the problem.

Within hours of sailing from Aalborg for the dubious delights of the North Sea in the Superiority I was standing in the skipper's cabin telling him I was going to pay off his ship in Glasgow, and could I please have my docking bottle.

As a ship's officer in a coaster I was entitled to a bottle of

Scotch duty free, but what I didn't know was that it was down to his discretion. He turned me down flat.

He burst into a tirade of personal insults into which I, my parents' marital status, and England, all came in for equal venom.

'Ye'll ne'er grace my ship again,' he screamed in raw and furious Scots. That did it - hanging grimly onto a stanchion as the ship sashayed her way back to Scotland - I went eyeball to eyeball with him.

'The only fing that will give this ship any kind of grace is a bloody torpedo' I yelled back in tortured Cockney. I was told later that our shouting match was heard clear through the ship.

The man never spoke to me again. Two days later we tied up in Glasgow and I was up on my toes and off down the gangplank, luggage, discharge book and cash in hand, heading for Kings Cross as fast as I could get there.

Whatever happened to the SS Superiority I never found out - but a year later her sister ship, whose name escapes me, went down in the Irish Sea with all hands.

I can recommend to Weight Watchers the onion sandwich diet. It may not be very social in terms of breath etc, but it worked for me. I should probably never have paid that ferryman but my sea-urchin career was over for good.

What would follow now would be the glue factory, Dearly Beloved and learning to be a grown-up.

40

National Service? Never done me no 'arm!

With hordes of young YOBs running the streets and teenagers getting knifed to death or even gunned down in their own homes, it's not hard to hear the growing crescendo of demands. *'Stick em in the army – it never done me no 'arm'*, as those of us of a certain age remember the lost years of our own youth.

To be fair, they do have a point though none of us would have admitted it at the time. It did broaden our horizons and thumped some elements of self discipline into us, though we'd tried everything from claims of flat feet, to *'sorry I can't hear you doctor'*, to get out of it.

At the end of the day we young lads were torn from the bosoms of our families – and the bras of our girl friends – to be turned into fighting machines. We would be coiled springs, killers ready to attack and kill the first Russian we came across outside an Olympic squad.

There were choices of course. You could dig coal for Britain, or go off to sea in the Merchant Navy until you were 36. Guess which wally did his national service, and then went into the Merchant Navy? In fact for most of us lads the real choice was a touch of khaki, a flash of air force blue or the swagger of bell bottomed trousers and jacket of navy blue.

Medicals, I hear you ask? Well, apart from making sure our eyes worked, we could fill a bottle on demand and coughed the right way when grabbed by the scrotum, the only other requirement at the Wanstead National Service centre appeared to be whether you could breathe in and out. Then, having been coughed, prodded and peered at from an odd direction, we all shuffled into the 'examination' room to be tested.

Suffice to say the toughest question on the paper was. 'What is your name?', but it did sort us out for the interviews. Most of the lads, having watched the RAF from fairly close quarters in their youth, said they fancied the air force. The army however, wanted shore-to-shore khaki, and laid claim to most of the cannon fodder as soon as it had been coughed and prodded.

The Navy? *'No chance, son, though we do have some landing craft in the army'*. There were, however, occasional exceptions and from time to time the Admiralty dipped its fingers into the pool of cheap labour offered to it by conscription, and that worked for me.

But they were very particular about who they did take and, steeped in naval tradition as it is, insisted that preference was given to those reluctant recruits who had family backgrounds with the senior service. Those of us who wanted to joined up by the navy - in preference to the Brylcream Boys and the Khaki jobs - had to frantically invent or produce relatives as evidence of the salt coursing through our veins.

Those with kin at Jutland or on the Russian Convoys during the last war had fairly good chances and as it happened I had both. A very elderly uncle had left the Navy after Jutland, and they had long since given up looking for him, while Uncle Syd had done his share of the runs to Murmansk.

It worked and before I left Wanstead I'd been assured I was just what the navy wanted and that my travel orders would be in the post. So it came to pass that on December

4th 1954 I found myself en-route to Cornwall and HMS Raleigh.

Three weeks later, just in time for Christmas, I was home again on leave with the best bird-pulling gear around. Bell bottomed trousers, blue collar, the works and as the old song says, 'all the nice girls love a sailor'

Took me months to realise it wasn't the nice girls we wanted.

41

Nothing like home cooking

I have already made a passing reference to school dinners (reminiscence 27) and how I was once challenged (well he said invited) by a local headmaster to write a piece for a paper I was working on about school dinners. I was on the governing body of his school at the same time as it happens so it was difficult to say no.

Now I have to admit that the prospect did not exactly fill me with any great enthusiasm, because my own schoolboy memories of that particular cuisine left me scarred for life. The meals came in the backs of county council vans with the main ingredients already plated up, with metal covers separating the food so they could be put into the steamer before being laid out ready to pick up.

Choices? For us it wasn't so much an epicurean experience as a safari through nausea, so when I arrived for the article on the appointed day (disappointed to be offered a cup of cheap coffee instead of a couple of glasses of headmaster's sherry as an aperitif) I was quite surprised to find myself in a queue of enthusiastic kids. It didn't take long to discover why.

Chips were on offer of course - they always are. But these were chips that looked like chips, chunky and sizzling fresh from the fryer – not melancholy sticks of limp potato. They were on offer along with specialities like quiche (which in my day would have been a spelling mistake), salads that looked fresh and crunchy, colourful vegetables and meat that didn't look old enough to have been shot by Robin Hood, as ours often seemed to have been.

What's more this magnificent menu was prepared and served by dinner ladies in the school – not delivered in the back of a county council van to be shoved into steamers. The food was laid out for individual selection, not just plonked onto plates a dozen miles away on a take-it-or-leave-it choice.

In fairness our school dinners were a boon to our hard-pressed parents who knew their children would be a hot and allegedly nourishing meal for about a tanner (two and a half pence in today's money) a time. Since we still had rationing at the time they also relieved a lot of the pressure on Mum's collection of ration-books, but we never appreciated such reasoning.

Remember Pom? They give it more attractively commercial names these days, but at least now it produces a reasonable facsimile of mashed potato. For us then it was the unappetising cornerstone of most of our school dinners, plopped onto the plate with an ice-cream cornet gadget.

After that came the gentle ladelling onto the plate of some peas that to be served carefully to stop them bouncing of it and the inevitable piece of meat pie. Well, I say meat pie but this had been constructed by the trayful using a filling of gravy-marinated gristle that had to be chiselled out of its tray to keep the peas and pom company. The whole production was drenched in a brownish watery liquid that got less brownish and more watery as the week went by.

Presumably it was to pander to any religious principles but on Friday we almost always had fish and chips. Well it was called that but to be honest Captain Birdseye would have walked his own plank rather than serve up what they gave us. However, smothered in layers of tomato sauce it at least brought a welcome change from the pom, peas and plaster pie.

Perhaps they were trying to condition us boys for the couple of years we would one day be eating Her Majesty's Pom – another experience in itself. Yes, we had the NAAFI to fall back on but even then twenty-eight bob a week (about £1.40) never bought a lot of steaks.

These days navy chefs have a great reputation for their food but I am not talking these days. Back then they had a great love of sauté kidneys on hardened toast or bouncy hardboiled (in steam) eggs for breakfast For lunch their minestrone soup had to be flavoured with vinegar while to follow, their version of cottage pie had all the texture of a thatched roof and the meat content of flavoured spam.

For tea it was always bread and jam, preparing for the main event of the day – supper, with dry roast potatoes, cabbage that came either overcooked or barely boiled accompanied by a slice of very dubious looking meat.

To be really honest navy food was not all that bad – at least it wasn't until the cooks got their hands on it and those of who spent more than a few hours on galley duty for some minor crime or other saw what they did. Naval chefs today might cook for royalty, but ours concentrated on meals that reminded you of home – 'just like mummy used to throw away', was the stock joke.

After all, we all know that there is nothing like home cooking, and that was just like the food the Admiralty's cook gave us – nothing like home cooking.

42

Don't they touch each other any more?

The thing we alleged wrinklies cannot understand about today's dancing is that the dancers seem to do little but face each other, surrounded by flashing lights and laser beams and wriggle about a bit. They can't whisper sweet nothings or murmur sensual invitations into each other's ears because of the ongoing and monotonous assault in their eardrums. What's the point of a great chat up line if you have to shout it?

There is, of course, the sad thought that the only way this form of tribal mesmerism works is with the help of murderous little chemicals down the throat or powder up the nose (which they have usually paid through the nose for as well).

What's wrong, kids? Why don't you touch each other any more? What was better than the salacious thrill of grabbing an armful of girl and spending the next five minutes in gleeful seduction, pressing and squeezing the places you could get arrested for pressing and squeezing out in the street?

Looking back now I guess we were a bit lucky. We'd survived the war and emerged into an adult world where we all had jobs and money to spend. On a mix of Senior Service, brown ale and the backseats of cinemas we lived life to the full, and that included the Saturday night 'hops'.

We would dance in Dagenham, rhumba in Romford,

seduce them in Seven Kings and get into punch-ups at the Palais in Ilford. In later years I often sipped a glass of ale in pubs that once banned us for life, but I think there was something about the 'Saturday night hops' that will never come again.

Crowds of gum-chewing local Lotharios, wearing yellow socks inside their crepe-soled shoes, peering around the Seven Kings Library hall to spot what was on offer. As Bill Birch or Kenny Ball (yes, the Kenny Ball) did the business with the Woodchoppers Ball they hunted in packs.

What they would see would be wall to wall girls – petitely seated on the chairs around the room wearing brightly coloured rayon frocks over starched petticoats – waiting for one of the ogling morons to pluck up his nerve. When one did he would squeak across the parquet flooring to make one of them an offer they couldn't refuse, in case it was the last one they got that night.

Most of us blokes thought all girls could dance anyway, and that it was a skill that came with the legs, whereas we never knew a foxtrot from a funky chicken. That was why we welcomed the simplicity of jive and rock n roll. We could just stand there shaking the odd leg, while the girl did all the twisting and turning. That bit I can still do - for a few seconds.

I guess the best bit came with last waltz time when you could really get up close and personal and the whispered persuasions about who sees who home that night. Many a romance began under that spinning shiny ball and the quiet tones of a clarinet.

Then, thanks to the government's insistence that we spent a couple of years learning to defend our country, our Saturday nights began to be spent more in dance halls and NAAFI canteens far from the 'smoke' (London). So the Cockneys had to relearn the arts of seduction in a dozen different dialects from Cornish to Geordie, but some of us had the bird pulling kit in the business.

Most of your nightclub wigglers today would never have experienced the joys of bopping in bell-bottoms, or having an armful of perfumed bosom snuggling up to a skin-tight navy suit as they waltzed to the erotic music of Acker Bilk in a Plymouth dancehall.

Thinking about it though, my most memorable Saturday night out like that was in a little Newfoundland 'town' called Port Union. This really was a tiny village on the coast of Newfie which apart from some fishing boats had very little going for it – but it did have girls. (It also had a brand new jetty until we pulled out of it a few days later and someone forgot to 'let go aft').

I was a Merchant Navy officer in the Fort Avalon by then and a few of us went ashore, in uniform of course, to see what a Saturday night out on the frontier was like. We were laden down with bottles of Scotch, packs of duty free fags and some other items I won't go into here, but were all good trade goods.

We found a store, well 'the store', with a small back room with one of those old fashioned woodstoves in the centre and a tiny bar in the corner. The room was already full when we arrived – well, there must have been at least twenty people there – and then the band turned up.

A couple of fiddlers, an accordionist and a bloke in a tartan shirt calling out the dance steps. Never got that at the Palais.

Eat your heart out Kenny Ball!

43

On the run

We've got a fig tree in our garden – acquired by Dearly Beloved some years ago and tenderly nurtured by her ever since. This year it exploded in blossom, which in the course of time turned into figs. Now I have to confess that, while I have eaten in restaurants all over the world, thanks to my mother I have never actually tasted a fig.

I have but distant and vague memories of the East Ham slum we moved out of, a week or two ahead of the Luftwaffe, into Becontree Avenue. The hazy memories do include those of an outside lav, with squares of newspaper nailed to the back of the door and a hole in the passage wall through which my mother could call her own mother who lived next door.

In the Avenue we had the luxury of an upstairs toilet, though to be fair we spent a lot of our early months at the end of the garden in the Anderson shelter, which didn't. There it was a case of using the old china gazunda (cos it gazunda the bunk) during the nightly visits of Goering's finest.

You would not think that in such circumstances any kind of laxative would have been necessary, but mothers then were very keen to ensure their brood was 'regular'. The old Radio Doctor, Dr Charles Hill, on the BBC used to advise the nation on health matters, always told us to 'keep regular'.

That meant the bowels being exercised daily, and flushed out once a week. For some it meant Senna Pods or Ex-lax, but our mother insisted on a Friday night spoonful of thick, black foul-tasting and evil-smelling Syrup of Figs.

We had a family routine every night at bedtime. My brother Roy and I, washed and in pyjamas (with overcoats close by in case the siren went) had to say our prayers. Yes, our agnostic parents, one an excommunicated Catholic and the other a disinterested Protestant, insisted on us going through the 'God Bless Mummy and Daddy' routine, that also included a plea for Him to look after grandparents, and Uncle John who was a prisoner of the Italians.

But on Friday nights there was the dreaded added extra, when she brought out the teaspoon and the bottle of SoF she'd bought from Timothy Whites. We would promptly vanish, cowering behind the settee and refusing to come out while she had that spoon in her hand. The more we cowered the more impatient she got and her arguments, which usually carried the pledge of a good whacking if we didn't come out, always prevailed.

We would edge nervously forward, mouth reluctantly agape to receive our weekly measure of the old bowel stimulus. Once within reach she would hold our head by the hair and jerk it backwards so she could force the liquid down our throats. We would cough, splutter and beg for some sugar or a fruit drop to take the dreadful taste away.

Boy did that stuff work! By Saturday morning we were too scared to run about too much, but when the Saturday Morning Pictures restarted after the war it became a race to make sure we could perform before it was time to leave for the Regent. Many years later she did relent when some chewing gum laxative came onto the market, and I remember Roy and me celebrating because she not only appeared to forget the SoF but even gave us some chewing gum.

The fact is that from those days onwards I never liked figs. Dearly Beloved, on the other hand, loves them and I have never envied her the fig rolls she keeps in the cupboard. Nor have the blandishments of Ready Steady Cook and other chefs over the years ever really changed my antipathy towards the figs; well, not until this year.

When I spotted a particularly plump fig preparing to drop off our fig tree, I determined that when it was ready I would at least try it and see what fresh fig actually tasted like. So I watched that particular fig getting bigger and plumper by the day and even began to look forward to tasting it by checking out some quite deliciously sounding recipes.

Sadly, the bloody birds she attracts into our garden with peanuts and other delicacies were thinking on the same lines. One of them got to it first.

44

They told Dad the error of his ways

One of my enduring family memories was a Christmas Day when the kids were small and, surrounded by the debris of used plates, empty bottles and the remains of a dead turkey, I happened to let slip about one of my earliest literary achievements.

'You did what?' a clearly disbelieving Tracey said and she wasn't alone in her doubting.

'I don't believe you.' Debbie our second eldest muttered, while the even younger David and Emma looked around the table, bewildered about the meaning of what I'd just told them.

Airily, still clutching the glass of Scotch that had barely left my hand that day, I repeated what I'd said. 'I once won a prize for a temperance essay'.

Their mother, choking as she tried to suppress her laughter headed towards the washing up sink. The brood, especially the older two, hoping the distraction would help them avoid helping their mother, were hysterically clutching their sides at the thought of their father having the temerity to write about the evils of drink.

But it was true. I really did once have a certificate verifying I had won a prize with a written condemnation of drink and the evils it brought upon the family and society in general. To be honest it could not have been that profound because I was only about eight at the time.

Although my father had been brought up in Wapping slums as a strict Roman Catholic and mum, from East Ham, loosely defined herself as CofE, it would be fair to say that neither had any strong religious beliefs. In fact Dad had once been visited by his priest in the East End who'd heard he was about to marry a Protestant and wanted to make him see the error of his ways.

As I understand it, that priest had been lucky to escape with his life – only saved because Dad's brothers held him down while he did.

In the Avenue we were awash with religion. A Catholic Church (and school), an Anglican one and even a Synagogue were all within easy reach. On Sunday mornings the Salvation Army banged their tambourines and squeezed their concertinas outside our house and the Boys Brigade blew their bugles down the Avenue on their way to church. We didn't know it of course but a mile or so up the road even a future Archbishop of Canterbury called George Carey, was raking the same streets we were.

Just around the corner was a Methodist church and that was where we were sent to give parents an hour or so afternoon's peace to Sunday School. To be fair they wouldn't have known the difference between a Methodist and a Moslem. There we would sit on tiny chairs, singing our little hearts out about twinkling stars and the baby Jesus, before taking home handfuls of scent cards (at a penny each) to make Mum's knickers drawer reek of lavender. We also had the annual Temperance Essay competition.

I really wanted to prove myself there, but initially had what we now call a touch of 'writers block'. I just couldn't come up with a topic, but dear old Dad was the inspiration.

He'd known all about poverty and going to school barefoot. He'd been part of one of the many large families living on scraps while the men (and sometimes the women) drank what little cash they did have, after going to Mass. True, Dad liked a pint as well, but he and mum had made up their minds from the start that their children would never suffer in the same way they had, so he never made a habit of it.

He enjoyed festivities and family parties like Christmas but he was never a boozer. He did, however, tell us many stories about that early life of his and how so many children suffered during those days.

So I wrote a heartrending piece about children suffering from drunken fathers who sometimes beat them up when they were in their cups. In truth I probably also drew most of the inspiration from the works of Charles Dickens, whose children's versions of Oliver Twist etc had made a deep impression. Probably, even plagiarised some of the great man's words without knowing I was doing it.

Anyway, I won and was duly presented with a book and the flamboyant Methodist Society certificate by a delighted minister. Problem was I think he read a little too much into it, and he turned up a few days later to talk to Dad about his drink problem.

I remember him being invited to leave rather hurriedly, and we were never sent to Sunday School again.

45

Well, it was Christmas after all

The first girl I ever slept with was my cousin, and just to make it a family occasion my brother and her sister were in bed with us at the same time. Well, it was Christmas after all!

OK, it was during the war and we were all under ten. The venue was either in our house or with aunts and uncles in theirs the following year. The usual worry was finding a chicken, and whether Father Christmas would chance his luck if it was a bombers moon on the most important night of the year.

For Dearly Beloved and me these days the day is usually a quiet evening at home watching a repeat of a Morecambe and Wise Christmas special and haggling over the tea-making; but I used to love those old family Christmases.

If it was out turn that year, at teatime aunts, uncles and cousins would arrive from all directions through the blackout wishing everyone in sight good cheer. The best room carpet would be taken up, in case some Mann and Crossman brown ale spillages stained it. Quart bottles of beer had been quietly piled up in anticipation in the larder for weeks, along with a bottle or two of smuggled gin and/or whisky that had arrived from unspecified sources and the bottle of Port gran had contributed.

Thanks to Mum's Family Christmas Loan Club money was no problem. She ran it with scrupulous integrity throughout the year, painfully extracting shillings and half-crowns from us each week. Many East End pubs had their own Christmas Loan clubs, but a lot of their organisers seemed to develop itchy feet and sticky fingers in November, so she preferred to do it herself.

The Christmas chicken always presented a problem of course, what with wartime rationing and everything. There were never very many strung up in the open air outside the butchers, as they used to be, but there were usually some reliable 'nod and a wink' bargains to be had.

Only once did we look like being birdless – even Dad's trip to 'the Lane' had seen him coming home without a bird in the hand (see reminiscence 26). Fortunately, or unfortunately as it turned out, Uncle Syd arrived home on leave from Chatham Barracks that Christmas Eve clutching one he'd sort of acquired somewhere in Kent.

It proved to be the sort of bird legends were made of – and foundation stones too, because it was the toughest piece of meat we'd ever stuffed. Dad thought so too after it broke one of his false teeth.

Not to worry. By the evening, once the relatives had arrived things really began to move. A few gin-and-oranges, a glass or three of booze, with us kids already burping Tizer and with one ear cocked for the air raid warning, the 'knees up' behind blacked-out curtains began.

The Irish bit was always big with us of course, despite being several generations away from the Paddies on Dad's side who'd left the Emerald Isle in the potato famine. Mum played the piano of course and we all got emotional about taking Kathleen home, the Mountains of Mourne and Danny Boy. To this day I can see my Dad, glass in hand and with emotional tears streaming down his face as he leaned on the piano singing about going across the seas to Ireland and Galway Bay. Not bad for a cockney from Wapping whose only experience of sailing anywhere was on the Woolwich Ferry.

A few 'Knees up Muvver Brown' jollies, hokey kokies and Lambeth Walks, with the festivities usually killed off with Vera Lynn's party-pooper, 'We'll meet again' and mum would produce the huge bowl of jellied eels she'd made for the occasion. Then, for the grown-ups it would be time to sit down and try to cheat each other out of pennies with hands of pontoon, before snoozing away in the armchairs.

By then we kids would be long in bed – girls at one end and boys at the other, topped and tailed like human sardines and ready dressed for the shelter, just in case the Lufwaffe sobered up enough in time to spoil things.

46

Woolies was finger-nicking good

Woolworths today is modernised, attractive and not so thick on the ground as it used to be when it offered opportunities for young people to learn the fundamental rudiments of crime. Well, at least it was until the whole shebang went bust and closed down all its stores anyway.

Even before it went belly-up, today's light-fingered 'artful dodgers' not only had modern displays and vigilant store detectives to deal with in those stores, but could even have found themselves starring on TV – and I don't just mean Crimewatch.

It was all so much easier in our day when Woolies was in every High Street and a treasure trove for booty wherever you happened to be. There you could pick up everything from clothes pegs and penny whistles to easily palmed bottles of Ashes of Roses scent. Its flat counters were divided into compartments displaying all the store's wares and sparsely supervised by a girl who also had to handle the till when kosher shoppers actually bought goods.

It never really mattered which Woolies you went into, because they were all the same but it was often safer to 'play away'. The one in Heathway was popular for example because, if you had to go up on your toes, there were always a lot of people outside passing by that you could lose yourself in without the risk of being recognised.

Truly every one of those stores was an urchin's paradise.

In them we could roam up and down counter-shopping (especially when it was raining outside), our eyes feasting greedily in the array of goodies laid out at our fingertips.

The cheap toy counter was the main attraction of course, though many a mum was happy to cough up a few pennies without asking questions for a set of new clothes-pegs we'd happened to find 'in the street'. Their consciences were eased because someone had clearly dropped them from their shopping basket and 'finder's keepers' was the general rule of thumb.

There were also times when we were sent there on genuine errands with actual money to buy goods. If you nicked them and pocketed the dosh instead no one was any the wiser. It helped of course if you had your mates with you to provide the diversionary tactics. They would ask the girl on the counter for help at one end while lightning fingers did the biz at the other end of it.

Nicking was practically a way of life. Scrumping apples did not always need a convenient tree or orchard because the greengrocer always had outside displays of temptingly crisp Cox's Orange Pippins to tempt a passing hand. In addition many an allotment holder was puzzled by the amount of carrots etc that failed to come up from his seeds. Even dogs were at it, nicking the odd dog biscuit from the sack outside the pet shop as they slunk by.

As far as our own biscuits went, there was none of this pre-packed plastic-wrapped nonsense. Grocers had them in tins so they could sell them by the weight and they were usually there by the counter to dip into as you queued by the bacon-slicer with mum's shopping list in hand. That was 'serve yourself' before the concept became legal and a lot of us often did so.

There was one grocer's shop in the Avenue that still lingers in the nostrils, mainly because of the overpoweringly pungent smell of cheese that hit you as you opened the door. Opposite the local synagogue, it was presided over by a lady of that religious persuasion. An enormous woman who could clearly not move fast, she sat at the end of the shop knitting as she waited for customers – just like those old girls must have passed the time waiting for the guillotine victims to turn up.

Her biscuit tins were also lined up along the counter and were a regular after-school challenge because, while her sightline included people standing up in the shop, she could not see the floor. So the trick was to open the door and slide into the shop on our belly so she couldn't see us even when we reached the custard creams waiting for us.

One day she spotted me, literally with my hand in the tin, but fortunately she was too big to run as fast as I could. These days I know how she felt.

47

I saw 'itler at the butchers!

I will never forget the day I saw Hitler outside the butchers. I was seven going on eight and it was, as Albert Trotter used to say, during the war when, although the actual Battle of Britain had been won, there was still plenty going on around us.

The most important part of my personal war effort was insisted on by my mum and it involved queuing up at the Valence Corner (Andrews Corner then) greengrocer for five pounds of King Edwards spuds for sixpence, and then going to the queue outside Parishes (the butchers), for a few sawdust sausages. It was in that queue that I saw him.

I admit I wasn't in the best of moods that day because mum had interrupted a very important 'gobs' (five stones) championship where I'd been taking Georgie Pickford to the cleaners. I'd protested of course, but mum did have a way with words and a very persuasive right hand so, clutching her old canvas shopping bag in one hand a bob (shilling) in the other, I trudged glumly up the Avenue, past Hitchman's Dairies, to the greengrocer's.

I wasn't in a better frame of mind when I finally got clear of the spud shop and joined the line outside Parishes, but I was jolted out of my anti-maternal mutterings when I spotted 'him' a couple of places in front of me in the queue. How he'd got into the country I will never know, though I dimly remembered hearing dad talking about another

German called Hess who had apparently parachuted in. And why come to Dagenham anyway?

He stood there bold as brass, bigger than me of course and wearing a scruffy brown jacket, but with that very unmistakeable Charlie Chaplin moustache decorating his upper lip. He even had his hair brushed over his forehead like all the cartoonists drew the Fuhrer.

I watched open mouthed as Adolf moved down the queue and passed into the butcher's shop where he bought some liver. Cunning move that, pretending to be an ordinary British shopper but I was still amazed that I was the only one in the queue that day who seemed to recognise him. I nudged a few women but no one took any notice or realised who was in the queue with them.

As he left the shop I decided to take action. Abandoning any thoughts mum had of cooking sausages for tea, I left my place in the queue and began to trail Hitler to his lair. Bag of potatoes still in hand and taking advantage of natural cover in shop doorways and house gateways, I tracked him all the way down Valence Avenue until he disappeared into a council house. I took its number and excitedly rushed home to report my discovery.

Mum was less than impressed. In fact she was a touch furious that I'd come home with the potatoes but banger-less, and she brushed aside my revelation that I had discovered that Hitler was living up the road. When he came in from work dad wasn't much better, being more interested in sending me up to 'Robbsies' for 'ten Weights or Woodbines' while he got his Home Guard kit on than listening to me.

Georgie Pickford did believe me though, and we kept watch on Hitler's Valence Avenue hideout for a couple of days but then it started raining and we abandoned our surveillance without seeing our man again. Gradually he slipped out of our minds and, I suspect, quietly made his way back to Berlin somehow.

No one ever did believe me but I know the man I saw was definitely Adolf Hitler or, thinking about it, could have possibly been Charlie Chaplin. In fact over the years only one person has ever believed me, and that was Elvis Presley when I bought some chips off him in Brentwood a few years ago.

48

No one kicked sand in our faces

There was a lot of regular advertising to brighten our post-war lives though clearly not as much or as sophisticated as today's. We had the 'Bisto Kids' tempting our taste buds, and whole shed loads of adverts for different cigarettes, with possibly the most honestly named being 'Turf', because that was what they tasted like.

In the boy's comics like Hotspur and Wizard we were challenged to 'confuse your teachers – learn to throw your voice' for only a tanner (sixpence). This was the advert Ken Dodd claims was what put him on the road to show business.

But the one that caught our urchin's eye the most, was found not just in the comics but also in most newspapers and magazines. One of the most intense advertising campaigns of its day, it highlighted the seven-stone weakling who had sand kicked in his face by a big bully who then walked off laughing like a drain with puny's girl friend on his arm.

So he sent off for, and learned the secret of, 'Dynamic Tension' – the muscle-building method of an Italian-American called Charles Atlas – and was soon knocking the bully's block off to recapture his girl friend. A renowned bodybuilding muscle man Atlas had himself allegedly once been a puny weakling. Then, by studying the sinewy movements of tigers and other animals, he developed the ideas that made him muscular, famous and very rich.

Even before puberty every young man hankers for bigger biceps and gets impatient for them to arrive. We, and especially the Mild Bunch, led very active sporting lives that kept us healthy, but not using the exercises that promised the level of muscle development that would keep the sand out of our eyes. Dynamic Tension seemed to offer the solution – but since we were all still at school we couldn't afford the course. We feared being laughed at if we asked parents for more pocket money to pay for it.

We were desperate though, and decided that we would take Mr Atlas up on his scheme, but wouldn't tell him that three of us were going to pool our pocket money and share his secret. So, on behalf of the three of us, I sent off the money off and made sure I was on hand when the postman came so my own parents never knew and kept the envelope sealed until we all met up that evening to read 'the secret'.

What Dynamic Tension turned out to be was using our own muscles to compete with each other. For instance, cupping our hands together we would then try to pull them apart, thus putting great stress on shoulders.

The whole 'secret' consisted of such exercises, all designed to develop one muscle or another. Full of enthusiasm and optimism, we entered into the spirit of things. For weeks in quiet moments and in private, we were flexing, pulling and pulling muscles in every direction - all with an eye on that sandpit, but without any clearly obvious muscular benefit. Then one day we made the mistake of going to the pictures and our dream was shattered.

I forget what the main film was, but what had an impact on us that evening was the newsreel that was always an important part of the programme in those pre-TV days. It often had snatches of news events like the cup final that we could never have seen ourselves, or of Winston Churchill going off on a cruise.

The newsreel we saw that week included a feature about a major court case going on in New York. I can't even remember what it was about, but what did electrify us was the sight of one of the main witnesses. It was Charles Atlas – yes the same muscle-building hero who'd pledged to teach us how to avoid having sand kicked in our face. Trouble was, he was in a wheelchair.

Somehow Dynamic Tension never seemed to be the same after that

49

The Ragamuffin Olympics

Its a few years away yet but all our politicians, from Tessa Jowell upwards, are getting excited about the 2012 Olympics. This is down to seeing how much of our taxes they can spend in order to enjoy the lavish hospitality that goes with it themselves.

It was very different in 1948 when a Dutch lady called Fanny Blankers-Koen cleaned up, winning what were probably rolled gold medals then in sprinting and hurdling, and when I won Guinness Gold at Gobs.

I hasten to add that this was the colloquial name given to 'five stones', which was a favourite urchin game because all you needed to do was find five pebbles, if you didn't have the time to nick the proper coloured squares out of Woolworth's.

We were ever gripped by the sporting events of the day. Wembley may have hosted the real cup final, but that weekend there were mini cup finals going on in every street in the land. When Bradman brought his cricketers to whitewash England, we gained our revenge using battered and shiny tennis balls (aimed at cracks in the pavement to give them swing), hand-carved wooden bats and pig-bins as wickets. We even fought battles over who supported Oxford or Cambridge in the Boat Race and God knows on what basis we made our choices.

We had no telly of course but the papers and the BBC on

the wireless did a grand job in enthusing us. So, when the Olympics arrived – hosted by a skint post-war nation whose own athletes trained on ration books – we all got excited. The Mild Bunch decided to have our own Ragamuffin Olympic games.

We drew up a list of events that included marbles, cigarette-cards, top-spinning, hopscotch, paving-stone leaps and of course the inevitable gobs. We also had 'field' events – catapult and slingshot hurling – and the 'fifty yard dash'. That was about the distance from the apple, trees behind Valence House that we scrumped, and the safety of the road if we were spotted and chased.

We even organised our own medals. Nothing like the austerity versions dished out to Fanny Blankers etc but meaningful nonetheless with gold, silver and bronze. They actually came from crown beer bottle tops, stealthily retrieved from the dustbins of the Winding Way social club and the local off licence.

The black and yellow Guinness bottle-top was our gold, Mackessons stout as I recall provided us with 'silverish' medals, while Mann and Crossmans brown ale bottletops had a bronze touch about them. All you needed to do was prize the cork from the back of the bottle top and use it to fix it to your jacket or shirt by jamming said shirt between bottletop and cork. We were all set.

Personally, though I say so myself, in those days I excelled in two areas – gobs and ciggie card games like topsy and 'knocksie-downsie'. The skill in the latter lay in flicking your cards – all pre-1939 and many featuring pre-war sporting or British Empire heroes of course – so that they either covered up your opponent's, or knocked some already set up against a wall, down.

For some reason I was pretty good at ciggie cards and, like the old riverboat gamblers, always had a pile of them in my pocket ready to be fished out and used. In fact before we were evacuated for a few months I was the undefeated 1944 Stevens Road Junior playground champion, but a year or so later I got sent to the South East Tech and had to put away such childish things. The 1948 Ragamuffin Olympics represented my comeback and showed I still had a winning flick or two.

I held my corner in gobs too, but as far as marbles went – rolling blood-eyes along the gutter to hit other marbles was never my strong point. Nor was leaping about from paving slabs or hurling slingshots, though we were well experienced in the fifty-yard dash and could hurl a mean stone with a catapult.

Kids now can see Kelly Holmes etc strutting their stuff on the telly, but they don't have to risk a good hiding from mum for getting their new trousers muddy playing football. And they certainly don't have to risk life, limb and another good whacking, by climbing over fences to pinch bottletops for their medals.

50

Bell-bottomed Christmas

A few years ago, on holiday in Cornwall, I got Dearly Beloved to take a photo of me outside HMS Raleigh in Torpoint. She just about managed it before a surly armed 'bootneck' (Marine) came over and very impolitely told us to go away. It seemed that some naval brass were about to arrive and they didn't want the likes of us hanging around the gate.

They were singing a very different tune on December 6th, 1954 when they couldn't wait to get me, in a truckload of new cannon fodder through those gates. That day a bloke in uniform, who hinted he'd been born out of wedlock, loudly harangued us telling he had the thankless job of making sailors out of us.

The thing most on our, dog-tired and travel weary (via a sequence of station and train bars) minds at that moment, was whether we would be home for Christmas. As he bellowed at us that afternoon it seemed extremely unlikely, which was why most of us had had our tearful farewell parties at home the previous weekend.

In fact when the invitation to take part in the defence of the realm had arrived a few weeks earlier, Mum had spotted that her eldest was leaving home only three weeks before Christmas. She had to be talked out of writing to the Admiralty asking for my arrival to deferred until 1955.

So, on that cold and dismal day in frozen Torpoint few of

us were harbouring any real thoughts about being home for the turkey and trimmings that year. Petty Officer Loudmouth almost burst a blood vessel when one of our number nervously raised the issue while he was in mid-shout.

'Ome?' He shrieked. 'Wot - are you bored wiv us already? Do you fink we went to all the trouble to pay your fares here so we could send you home again. You will not even leave this camp until you have your uniforms and you ain't even been measured for them yet, so don't get your hopes up that you will be seeing mummy soon.' He was a man of few words, all of them bellowed and most of them profane.

It was true that most of HMS Raleigh would be closed for the Christmas fortnight but we would be too busy to worry about that, and he was dead right about the uniforms. We were about to be issued with the best 'bird pulling' clobber in the Palais, but had probably arrived too late to take advantage of it. It was a gloomy moment.

Next day we were issued with our kit - work clothes, boots, bits of uniform like the big deep blue collars (that had to be scrubbed vigorously to get some of the blue out of them so the wearer would look like he'd got some sea time in), and our kitbags and hammocks.

They also measured us up for the bell-bottom trousers and jackets of navy blue but it was doubtful they would arrive in time, let alone actually fit. Unlike the army battle-dresses they had to be skin tight and pulled on over your head (which was a bit difficult once your jabs had started working on your arms.)

Miserably we buckled down to basic training, slipping and sliding on the ice-covered parade ground with WW1 rifles rubbing our shoulders raw, polishing our new boots and being indoctrinated into Nelsonian tradition. Cornwall is a lovely county to visit in the summer... but you try square-bashing in it during an icy December.

All the time Christmas was getting closer. Frankie Howerd came down to entertain us in the camp theatre, but we couldn't even get tickets for that and there was no word on our uniforms. Our evenings were spent morosely drinking brown and mild and stuffing ourselves with pork pies in the teasingly decorated NAAFI.

The days ticked by, Loudmouth got louder and our arms got sorer from the rifle drill and inoculations. Our Civvy Street dosh was almost gone and all around us were other 'students' of previous intakes, preparing to go home for a Christmas which for us was looking pretty bleak.

Then suddenly the uniforms turned up and Loudmouth told us that we could go home – provided we passed haircut muster and had all our badges etc sewn on correctly. We sewed like mad and begged the barber to shear us.

Then, incredibly, we were back on the train swapping our boring HMS Raleigh cap-bands for the more exotic HM Submarines (quietly acquired through black market naval sources), and back in Dagenham with just days to spare. Then after Mum's tears of welcoming joy, it was free booze in the Royal Oak and the New Year dance where my waltz suddenly developed a sailor's rolling gait.

It had been a close run thing though.

51

Pope Jim

I guess to most people my Dad was just one of the London Transport 'chauffeurs' who drove them to work in his 145 or 148 bus between Ilford, Chigwell and Dagenham Dock for years until he retired. I say retired, but he worked for another ten years in a Boots warehouse in Stratford.

Few of his passengers in those days would have known that for one tiny period of his life, in order to get some new shoes, their driver was in fact the Pope. Well, at least he was in the annual Roman Catholic procession that wound its way through the Wapping slums sometime during the Great War.

Now, if there was one phrase that used to get dad angry, it was when someone referred to the 'good old days'. As he was at pains to point out, as far as the slum kids of the East End were concerned at the start of the 20th century there was nothing good about them. Normally a good-humoured man, he was very bitter about how they were hungry, ragged and barefoot in those 'good old days' when being part of a Catholic family meant sharing poverty with a dozen or more brothers and sisters.

His world had been one of pawnbrokers, taking family stews down to the bakers on Sunday to be cooked while parents were in the pub (after church) and all the dirt and filth that life in the slums meant. I used to doubt his stories of going to school barefoot until I saw photos of barefoot and scruffy kids taken in the East End at the time.

It had been the priestly promise of a pair of shoes that made him volunteer for the annual church procession, and for some reason he was chosen to be the Pope in one of the tableaux. I can well imagine my devout (if often drunk on gin) gran, 'Battling Biddy', weeping with emotion as she watched her eldest parading through Wapping that day.

Dad never had much time for the church. When the news got out in the street that he was about to commit the cardinal sin of marrying a protestant, his parish priest hot-footed to the Juniper Street tenement where the family lived.

Trying to bring 'Pope Jim' back into the Vatican fold he made some very injudicious remarks about 'mixed marriages', including that any children would almost be illegitimate. As I understand it Dad's brothers had to hold him down, while the priest rapidly made himself scarce.

Even as a kid Dad had been bitter about living on scraps of food and pawnbroker money while both Biddy and Dan (granddad) spent most of what little money he had in the pub. He was never impressed about them going to Mass on Sunday, and then straight into the boozer while the dinner was cooking in the local baker's oven. She'd acquired the name Battling Biddy because of her fiery Irish temper and tendency to indulge in the odd punch-up with neighbours when in her cups.

For obvious reasons, during the Hitler war many people went to church and we had no shortage of them around the Avenue – Catholic, Anglican, Methodist and even a Synagogue. My brother Roy and I were sent to Sunday School in the Methodist round the corner, presumably to give Mum a break but it was never a big thing.

Later on, in the Navy, I was often a Catholic (or Jew). After Sunday 'divisions' in shore bases like HMS Hornet, once we had been inspected the order was always given 'Jews and Catholics fall out', while the chaplain held a service for the CofE's. There would be an immediate outbreak of religious fervour as the NAAFI lovers of Rome and Israel went up on their toes.

But, even though he was an excommunicated outcast the one-time Pope Jim always insisted that we all decamped from Dagenham back to Wapping on Procession Day. There we would cheer the children in their finery as, shepherded along by solemn nuns, they marched with their banners past the bombsites just as they had done when Dad had been the leading light sometime back in the Kaiser's war.

Then we would all go back to Gran's flat in Stepney to feast on shrimps and winkles washed down with thick tea lightened up with pasteurised milk. They would all reminisce about past processions, and particularly about 'Pope Jim's' big day.

Apart from weddings and funerals however Dad always gave the Catholic Church – well any church to be honest - a wide berth. We had a Catholic school near us in the Avenue, but after his own apparently brutal experiences as a child there was no way he was going have his kids taught and beaten up by nuns and priests.

After developing a kidney problem that was affecting his brain and lucidity in his seventies, Dad spent his last days in Oldchurch Hospital. A normally fit man he had never really come to terms with losing my mother a year earlier, but this took us all by surprise.

He was clearly near the end but fighting it and they even wanted me to authorise turning off the machines keeping him alive. It was something we had great difficulty coming to terms with as a family but I had steeled myself to let them do it after one more weekend. Then, a few days before I was due to do so I visited him and he was particularly rambling in mind and tongue but I spotted a catholic priest coming down the ward and asked him to do what he had to do.

I still cannot believe what happened when that man went into his last rites routine. Even though it had been over sixty years since he'd seriously been to church, from somewhere in the recesses of his fevered mind Dad began to slur the responses. It was one of the most incredible experiences of my life, to see that man after all those years in denial, unmistakeably though incoherently saying the right things.

When the priest finished, I thanked him and casually told Dad I would see him the next day. Then, his voice as clear as a bell, he thumbed at the departing priest and said. 'Yeah, but don't bring him with you'. I grinned and nodded that I wouldn't as I waved goodbye, still chuckling.

A few hours later the hospital called me but before I could get back there he died; but bless him, Pope Jim had left me laughing.

52

Head over heels for Pet

I once had a very steamy passion, literally falling head over heels in love, for Petula Clark. Then it all evaporated when I saw the look on her face as she stepped over me and walked away.

Don't get me wrong – I have remained a lifelong fan of the singer who went on to even greater things after we both grew up. But we never met again after that fateful Saturday morning when she was simply a child-star prodigy and I a local urchin.

Back in the late forties and early fifties, Pet was being hailed as Britain's answer to Shirley Temple, having already made a number of very successful films as well as singing and acting on the West End stage. I seem to remember that at the time she was also working for the British Film Foundation, or some such nationalistic body making films fit for children to see. As part of that she used to carry out publicity personal appearances to cinemas.

One of these tours included the Odeon Saturday Morning Pictures Club. Remember, *'we come along on Saturday morning, greeting everybody with a smile... '* etc? We all promised to be *'good citizens when we grew up and champions of the free',* before settling down to a couple of hours of Donald Duck, Laurel and Hardy and a Bowery Boys cliff-hanger or our favourite cowboy Hopalong Cassidy

Petula, who was promoting her latest children's film, was touring those Saturday Morning Cinema clubs. There, to a noisy background of impatient shouting and cheering kids, anxious to get on with watching L&H, she would be introduced by the manager, say a few words and be handed a big bouquet of flowers. Then she would exit up the aisle to a torrent of enthusiastic applause and a standing ovation by a suitably impressed mob.

One Saturday she came to the Regent, in Green Lane (now a church or mosque or something similar I believe). We could hardly believe that such a big star as she was even then, although barely a teenager, coming to visit our humble little fleapit which wasn't even one of the posher ones like they had in Ilford. At the age of just eleven or twelve however, I had already been smitten and was deeply in love despite her being a few years older than myself. I was in love without even knowing what it meant.

Then I made the mistake of telling the Mild Bunch of that unrequited love and how I intended to declare it to her that morning. I was quite excited when we finally got into the Regent that day. I engineered myself a seat on the aisle I hoped my love would pass through on her way out, but I hadn't really noticed that one or two of my 'pals' had grabbed the seats right behind me.

It all went perfectly. Petula was introduced on the stage, did her bit, took her flowers and began to lead the parade of ushers and managers up my aisle towards the exit and her waiting limo. I was planning to call out to her as she reached me. But when she was but yards away from me I felt a violent shove in the back that propelled me out into the aisle and into 'her' path.

Unable to stop, I managed to roll over onto my back just as she reached me. She paused, looked down at the short-trousered ragamuffin prostrate before her, and her top lip curled up in disdain. Then she stepped carefully around me and led the procession away out into the foyer as I was seized, shouting that I loved her, but she never looked back.

Afterwards the cinema manager read me the Riot Act and threatened to tear up my membership card, and then I had a fight with the geyser who'd pushed me. From that day to this, I have never bought a Petula Clark record or a ticket for one of her shows.

No woman treats me like that and gets away with it matey!

53

We wore the luggage labels

We moved to Becontree Avenue in 1940, just a few weeks before the Luftwaffe turned our house in East Ham into a pile of rubble and we saw all the action from there. Well, with a short break in 1944 we did.

In March that year my sister Pat was born and, although we weren't losing as much sleep as we had during the blitz, my mother finally agreed with Dad that she ought to get us kids out of it for a while. Apart from the fact they had a new member of the family to consider, Hitler had started to keep us on our toes with his pilotless bombs (doodlebugs). While we kids were entertained by watching them pass by (hopefully) overhead, it was clearly not doing mum's nerves much good.

In fact I have always argued that the doodlebugs were much worse than the rockets Werner Von Braun designed to pepper us with later that year. With the V2s you never heard them coming until the explosion, but with the V1s you had that dreadful ten second pause, between hearing the engine stop and the big bang that signalled that someone else had copped it.

So it was that, sometime in the early summer, Dad took us all down to a local school where a fleet of buses was waiting for us. Mum was weeping with Pat sleeping in her arms and Roy and I stood, gas masks slung carelessly over our shoulder and wearing the now famous luggage-labels identifying us as evacuees.

Dad kissed us all goodbye, ordered his nine-year old eldest son to take care of his mum and help her with Roy, and I remember very clearly how he turned and strode away without a backward glance. It wasn't until years later that he admitted to me that he hadn't done so because he was crying his eyes out. (In those days real men did not cry, you understand).

I helped mum carry the few bits and pieces we had with us onto one of the buses, and we were taken to Barking station. There we were handed a packed lunch, of fish-paste sandwiches and an apple, before getting on a train for our mystery tour, because nobody knew where we were going. It proved to be a long and wearisome journey with many stops along the way, and a lot of rumours about our destination.

At one stage we saw a railway station – Oldham I think – where it looked like the mayor himself was waiting to greet us, but we rattled by. Eventually, that evening we stumbled off the train onto a platform where we were met by a lot of kindly ladies all talking like Gracie Fields and proffering cups of tea for the weary mums and orange juice for us dog-tired kids.

They ushered us onto more buses that took us to a big hall where they doled out some plates of stew and potatoes, before handing us blankets to settle down for the night. It turned out we were in a Lancashire mill town called Accrington and the next morning, after a breakfast of watery porridge, we became part of the 'cattle market'. Crowds of people came during the morning, inspected us closely and made their choices of who they wanted billeted with them.

We were one of the bigger families but Mum had made it very clear that in our case it was all or none. She would not have us split up, and if they could not find somewhere for all of us they would have to put us back on the train for London again. As things turned out we got really lucky. A wonderful lady called Mrs Broughton, the widow of a mill owner, came up to mum and asked if she would be prepared to help out in the house in exchange for her taking us in.

Mum said of course she would and before we knew anything we were in a real big posh car being transported to this ladies house in, wait for it, Oswaldtwistle. I say house, but it was more of a big manor house called Stanhill Villa that overlooked a farm and fields that stretched in a patchwork as far as the eye could see. We'd never really seen anything like it – there were cows and sheep in all directions, horses pulling ploughs and a styful of pigs down the lane. There was something else too.

Next to the house, in the lane, there was a long low and clearly very old building that reminded us of the air raid shelters we were used to in London. Its walls however were very useful as a football goal and cricket stumps, as well as just banging tennis balls up against it.

I wasn't until many years later that, on holiday with Dearly Beloved, I went through Stanhill for old time's sake and saw the building was still there. Furthermore it now had a bronze plaque screwed to it. It said that it was the very building where in 1764 James Hargreaves had invented the Spinning Jenny that played such a major part in the industrial revolution.

I loved Lancashire – we even went to Blackpool for the day, but we would only stay there for a few months before coming back to Dagenham.

I went to a local school, where I was always getting into fights because of my cockney accent, played in fields and paddled in local streams catching tiny frogs. Because of the friendship I struck up with the farmer's daughter, (no jokes please), I even worked on the farm down the end of the lane – learning to milk cows and helping bring in the harvest. It was the most amazing summer of my life up to then.

But in the end the strain of being separated from the old man was too much for Mum and she decided that, doodlebugs or not, we would come home. The D-Day landings had taken place and word had it that the doodlebugs were nothing like as regular as they had been, so she brought us home.

Just in time for the V2 rockets.

54

On yer bike

I get the impression that for today's kids the words 'pocket money' appear to be their share of the family budget, for which they have to do little more than hold out their hand, or hand over their mobile phone top-up card to be refilled.

It's true that we don't see too many milkmen needing help on our streets these days, and the only 'paper boy' I've seen down my way lately has been a 70-year old supplementing his pension.

For us every newsagent had delivery rounds and the United Dairies milk depot (and stables) in Bennetts Castle Lane always had kids outside in the early morning, waiting to pounce on a 'milkie' who might be in need of help. In our part of the Avenue we had 'Robbsies'.

The shop is still there but back then it was not just a newsagent and tobacconist – two or three days a week it was also a chippie behind the main shop. Run by the Robinson sisters – one of them very frightening, the other a kindly soul – they also had a meek and mild brother called (as far as I can remember) Tommy, who just did as he was told by his sisters.

They offered me the chance to make a few pennies delivering morning, and evening, papers. For the morning papers I had two rounds – a short one in the Avenue that included Dad's Daily Herald (and News of the World on Sundays) as well as my own Wizard – and a second longer and more complicated one through a network of nearby streets.

For doing these rounds, winter and summer seven days a week, I received the princely sum of 12-bob (60p) a week and the occasional Caley Tray chocolate bar as a bonus. Mind you when I go to get my own Sunday papers these days, I am very glad I no longer have to trudge around the streets with one of those big bags on my shoulder.

To be honest despite the eldest's fearsome appearance both the sisters were a kindly pair of souls and always keen to ensure their paperboys (never girls in those days) were happy and comfortable. When the winter winds blew they always insisted on stuffing brown paper down our chests to help keep the chill out, and if it was raining made sure we were wearing our school caps before we ventured out.

I did own a second-hand bike which I planned to use on the second round but sadly I padlocked it outside the swimming baths in Valence Park one day, where I was swimming in a Scouts gala, and someone nicked it – padlock and all. So I was not in a good mood when I turned up at Robbsies, late because I'd overslept, the next day.

'Never mind, Brian. You can borrow Tommie's', big sister Robinson told me. Tom, poor little browbeaten sod, handed it over and I wobbled away on it.

Now this bike was a boneshaker but it did the job. I would arrive in a street, park it on the kerb while I delivered the papers in that road and then move on to the next road to repeat the process. As I did so I was remembering my ex-bike, and cursing the geyser who'd taken it and what I'd do to him if I ever caught up with him. I found myself shoving the Times, Mirrors and Daily Sketches through letter boxes with a venom they didn't deserve, and never even paused to read the back sports pages like I usually did.

Finally I shoved the Times into the doctor's surgery in Green Lanes and made my way back to Robbsies to hand my bag in. Boss sister looked up as I walked into the shop and looked at me quizzically.

'Everything alright, Brian?'

'Yes thanks,' I grunted, handing over my bag before dashing home to get ready for school.

'So where's Tommy's bike?

Only then did I realise I'd parked the bike somewhere but then completed my round without picking it up again. Even worse, I could not remember where I'd parked it, so poor old Tommy had to tour the round to find it.

He never lent me his bike again.

55

We buried the milk in the garden

I was doing the weekly Tesco run with Dearly Beloved when, anxious to be of help, I picked up a packet of streaky bacon and tossed it into our trolley. With the kind of typical shake-of-the-head glare that women love to use when shopping with their, (ahem), better halves, she looked at the 'sell by' date and tossed it back onto the shelf.

It wasn't actually out of date but would have been within a few days. Her reasoning was that, by the time we actually came to eat it (or me actually, since she's a strictly Shredded Wheat breakfast girl) it could have been.

That's the kind of world we live in today – where instead of having our rashers cut from the bacon slicer to order, we take our chances on a plastic vacuum-wrapped pack. This not only gives us every detail, apart from the name of the ex-pig that provided it, but even tells us when we can't eat it any more.

There was a time when Tesco was a little store like the Home & Colonial and where Sainsburys was more famous for its big marble-topped counters and queues at every section. We bought our butter, or 'marge', at one counter and watched it being weighed, patted into shape and wrapped in greaseproof paper, before being handed over. Then we moved to the other counters of the shop to queue up again for our loose (or broken) biscuits, pots of jam or marmalade and our eggs.

We may have lived off ration books, but what we did eat was at least fresh and we never topped up the landfill sites with plastic. The only indication of a 'sell by' situation was a wrinkled nose when you smelt it as you got it out of the larder. In summer the butter (or National Margarine) melted in the butter dish, while in winter you had to almost chisel it onto the bread. In either case no one could smear it onto the bread as thinly as my mother who didn't so much spread it, as discolour the slice with it.

She could also wield the bread knife with tremendous accuracy. She could cut your regular 'tin' loaf in such thin slices it was practically 'see through buppy'. In winter she did let up a bit and cut toast size slices thick enough to hold on a fork in front of the fire

Keeping food fresh was always a problem. Like other houses in the Avenue we had a 'larder' but apart from having a flyproof shuttered window, its only cooling asset was the inevitable marble shelf. The only people with fridges were the ice cream shops, butchers and those lucky enough after the war to get a prefab that included a fridge. The idea of freeze-dried or frozen goodies would have been the stuff of science fiction, if it hadn't been too ridiculous an idea even for that.

Our milk was delivered (sometimes with that bonus of manure deposited by the UD horse outside a lucky gate) every day including Sunday. In a bad winter that could result in the stuff being frozen on the doorstep but in the summer it presented problems keeping it from going sour (and protecting it from the tits who could peck the tops off bottles with ease before you got up).

I remember our Mum getting her hands on an earthenware pot into which she poured the milk and, after covering it to keep any dirt out of course, buried it up to its neck in the garden. Then throughout the day she would water the earth around the pot in an effort to keep it cool.

What's more it seemed to work, not just with the milk but with the marge too.

She also taught us kids a trick I often use to this day – before frying an egg she would break it into a cup. That way she made sure that if the hen fruit was a bit over-ripe, (as it often was) at least she could toss it down the drain and not have her frying pan in need of a deep clean.

56

The age of innocence,
shoplifting and scrumping

One of the saddest headlines I saw recently was a report – and we get more of them these days than from a machine gun – saying that 25 percent of children under ten are not allowed to go out to play on their own. In other words we are robbing young people of an essential part of their childhood by preventing them learning how to play together.

Don't get me wrong, I fully understand why. When there have been so many high profile cases of children being snatched, abused and even murdered, parents are naturally scared to let them out of their sight. The fault is not theirs, but of the vicious world we live in where children kill children and evil men seek them out to satisfy their perversions.

Yet my world was violent too - we had Hitler trying to kill us during the unpleasantness with Germany, and after that the razor gangs, 'cosh boys' and 'the Teds' often made eye-catching headlines that showed we had a few social problems too. Like today's kids we were *'bored, cos there's nuffing to do'* despite the youth clubs, swimming pools, parks, libraries, cinemas and dance halls we had on offer and which still exist.

Despite all that I don't remember a time, either during or after the war, when we kids were kept indoors. Even before school age we were playing outside in the street. Mind you we did have some advantages like the narrow woodland (the bushes) that stretched along the centre of the Avenue, and the reassuring presence of a local copper called Lusher (who we kids hated) living in our street. We also had very little traffic to speak of so even living on a dual carriageway was no real problem.

The fact is we grew up learning to relate to, and respect, each other by playing games in 'gangs'. But our 'weapons' were football boots and cricket balls used in friendly combat, not knives to plunge into other kid's chests in fights. Yes, we all carried knives – but they were small penknives used to cut string, carve initials in trees or take the stones out of horse's hoofs. A little older and some of us even carried the sheath knives on our belts that formed part of our scout uniforms.

For us mobile phones and computers were the science fiction of the future. Today we live in that 'futuristic' world, but they're misused because the self-discipline we learned in short trousers is not possible today. Today we are afraid to let the kids out of our sight.

And that's the big difference. Our mums were only too pleased to see the back of us in the early morning, provided we were back before dark or for teatime, whichever came first. We raked the streets, did a bit of shoplifting in Woolies, scrumped apples from the trees behind Valence Library, threw stones at the ducks in Barking Park and played 'knock down Ginger' in roads where we weren't known.

In many ways it was an age of innocence where it was exciting to catch a glimpse of a girl's knickers as she stood on her hands against a wall, though we never knew why it was exciting. By the time we did find out, it was too late.

Learning street wisdom that way did have some dangers though, because sometimes we picked up words we didn't always understand. When I was about five I remember mum sitting me on the draining board to scrub my knees. While she was doing that I amused myself bursting the soap bubbles in the bowl and when one escaped my probing finger I called it a 'little b.....'

She looked up from my knees and asked me what I'd said. When I repeated it, she gave me one of the biggest hidings I ever got and believe me she packed a hell of a right hand. See, lesson learned; but I never found out who taught me the bloody word in the first place!

57

The day peace broke out

Music hall comedian Robb Wilton always opened his wartime performances on the wireless with, 'the day war broke out...' before launching into a long and very funny monologue. I was reminded of it when I glanced at the calendar and saw it was May 8th – the day peace broke out back in 1945.

People used to say they knew exactly where they were on the day John Kennedy died – well those of us around at the time knew exactly what we were doing on May 8th 1945. The schools were closed for the day in anticipation of the event and the Mild Bunch was having a tennis-ball kick-about in our part of the Avenue. Then my father came out of the house and called my brother Roy and I to come home.

Bit annoying really, because I was just about to do my Stanley Matthews bit and dribble the ball through the cracked paving stones en route to the lamppost and pig bin we were using for the goal that day. However I knew better than to play the old man up, so gloomily we trudged into the house, leaving the others to play.

Now our dad may have been a poorly educated Cockney from Wapping, who'd got most of his learning out of the old Daily Herald, but he had a deeply instinctive sense of occasion. He wanted all his family to be there when peace was declared because he felt that it was an historic moment his children should experience.

We got indoors to find them standing by the wireless in

the front room - Mum, Dad and Granny Lacey (who lived with us), clutching tiny glasses of carefully hoarded sherry. Suddenly we heard the unmistakable voice of our leader, the Prime Minister, telling us it was all over and that we could put the gas masks and tin helmets away at last.

I think it was one of the only times I ever saw my father cry as he and the womenfolk tearfully raised their glasses to toast 'peace'. It was clearly a highly charged emotional moment for them – and a highly frustrating one for me, because I could hear the lads outside still scoring. It was what happened next though, that I remember most of all.

Once they'd finished hugging and kissing each other indoors, we all trooped outside just as all our neighbours were coming out as well. I suppose in retrospect it was the first time I really knew the meaning of the word 'community', because men and women were shaking hands, hugging and kissing everyone that passed by. The people on the other side of the avenue were pouring over to our side to join the celebration, though the men were clearly also about to head off towards the Royal Oak in Green Lane or the nearest off licence.

For us, the football was no longer even possible with the amount of people-snogging going on all over the pavement, but we soon had another distraction. A few of the grown-ups began to build a bonfire at the Avenue's junction with Winding Way and we kids were recruited to collect anything burnable. We also had to create a 'Hitler Guy' to put on top of the fire.

In the weeks to come we would enjoy street parties and homes would be festooned with notices welcoming home various members of the family. Peace was something of a new experience for us kids but even adults were carried away by the general excitement.

That first night of peace bonfires lit the night sky in the streets all around us. On ours we burned our effigies of

Adolf because now they were our fires and not his. We stuck potatoes into the embers of the fire to be retrieved later and tossed more wood onto it when it started to die down. Some fools even threw their ration books into the flames without knowing it would be years before they would not be needed again.

Where people got all the booze from, heaven knows, but that night even PC Lusher, the neighbourhood rozzer, was unsteady on his feet. Community spirit took on a whole new meaning that night. Everybody loved everybody and I have no doubt that the bushes and trees that ran down the middle of the avenue in those days provided cover for many a drunken neighbourly seduction in the dark.

Winston

We were too young to understand, at first.
Oh, we knew there was a war
We'd often heard the Luftwaffe cursed
Above the bombs and ack-ack roar.

To us kids the Blitz was adventure
Though our parents did know fear
Night after night, being ever unsure
If it was to be our last one here

But they had a secret weapon – a voice
And when it spoke they listened.
It told of history, tradition, freedom, choice
Blood was summoned, sinews stiffened

He sent the English language into war.
Growled defiance, praised 'the Few'
Touched every single British core
People stood taller – spirits raised anew

He offered only blood, tears and sweat
Came out to shattered streets on tour
So giving renewed strength to all he met
And proclaimed it was, 'our finest hour'.

'We will fight them on the beaches
In the streets, fields and in the hills'
His words went out and reached
The very soul of British wills.

'Let the Nazis do their worst',
He declared, during desperate days
As our own teams were dispersed
To go, and 'set Europe ablaze'.

I remember well, that eighth of May
Dad called us in from in the street
To hear that voice again, but now to say
Its peace, thank God – Hitler's beat

Older by that time we kids knew more
About this very great Englishman
Who'd led and inspired us through the war
With words, 'V' signs and cigar in hand.

Then one day the grown ups went to vote
Now they wanted their brave new world.
So they threw the skipper off the boat
And so his battle flag was furled.

Yes, he was gone from Number Ten
But in the halls of power still heeded
The voice now spoke of an Iron Curtain
Warning that caution was still needed

Naked Knees and Blakey'd Boots

A few years more, and he was back in charge
Feebler, vaguer, yet still Britain's voice
Speaking now against the Commissars
Still preaching liberty, equality and choice

When the people heard that he was so ill
They waited in the street outside
Quietly murmuring, as they kept silent vigil
Praying, through tears as the great man died

In Westminster Hall he lay in state
As grateful thousands paid their dues
God knows, what might have been our fate
Without this man, who dared not lose

Of course his funeral was one of State
Magnificent words under St Paul's great dome
With Royals, Presidents, the good and the great
Then upriver to his final chuchyard home

We lined the City that day in our last tribute
Muffled drums, the slow procession passed
London's dockers dipped their cranes in salute
To the flag-draped casket behind the mast

He was a legend whose years we'd shared
Artist, author, statesman of destiny
Our defiant shield, a man who'd dared
And we'd walked with him through history

Brian Lynch

58

Cream cakes and the latchkey kids

Back in the immediate post war days when London Transport had whole fleets of red double-deckers clogging up the roads, the morning rush hour was a bleak time of day. From 7am they would be filled by bleary-eyed men coughing their way to work on Old Holborn smoke-filled upper decks towards Fords - the buses weaving their way through streams of push-bikers pedalling up the hill through Heathway.

Then, a couple of hours later, the tide would be renewed when, having got the kids off to school, hundreds of mums travelled the same buses but this time going towards Ilford and the sprawling Plessey factory. Once there they would sit in great lines soldering pieces of electronics together to make telephones, radios and gramophone decks, until 3.30pm when they would chatter and clatter over the long railway bridge between Ley Street and Ilford High Rd to get the bus home.

Now usually the kids would get home from school before they did and that left the problem for most of how they were to get into the house. Easy – they hung a key behind the door on a long piece of string so it could be reached through the letter box. Thus we became known as the 'latchkey kids'.

Nowadays of course nobody would even dream of hanging a key within easy reach for any light-fingered scallywag that happened along, but then it was a natural thing to do. I would guarantee that there were whole streets of open invitations to visit while the folks were out but it was very seldom taken up other than by the families involved.

It wasn't until after the war that Mum decided to help the family finances out by getting a part time job. Plessey was screaming out for women, whose delicate fingers were suited to that kind of work and they recruited them by the score. There were three of us kids by then and the sort of dosh London Transport paid the old man to take people to and from Fords wasn't exactly over-abundant.

We had Granny Lacey (her mum) living with us so she looked after the toddler Pat, but as a backup when Roy and I came back from school there was the latchkey solution. Looking back now, being a latchkey kid was a very important part of our lives. The extra cash she earned helped us keep up with the lot next door, put better lino on the floor, eat shop-bought cakes and have our butter spread thicker on the bread.

As far as the cakes were concerned Friday night was always a bit special in our house because she spent some of her wages on some marvellous fresh 'cream' cakes in the Plessey canteen to bring home as a treat.

There were other advantages about her working there too. When I was a teenager she had the chance to buy an automatic eight-record gramophone deck made in the factory. We had to provide our own casing for it but when we did and got it wired up, we found it never changed the bloody records anyway. She did complain but had it pointed out to her that when staff bought rejects, they always took a risk. It looked impressive though.

For years mum and her mates clattered over that bridge (sometimes on Dad's bus when his conductor would forget to take her fare), and life as a latchkey kid was great. Then disaster struck. One night she came home in tears with the sad news that her assembly line had been 'laid off'. Tragedy – yes, our brand new nine-inch TV was paid for, but it was the end of the line for the cream cakes.

Thankfully a few weeks later Plessey won a new contract and wrote to all the women who had been laid off begging them to come back again. So we had the cakes back and the front door key went back on a string behind the door again.

59

I wish I'd looked behind me

Today we have television and DVDs but none of them have the attraction of the old cinemas – those wonderfully splendid emporiums of escapism. Drawn to them by the derring-do of Errol Flynn and the road-worthy antics of Hope and Crosby for us they had other attractions for hot-blooded teenagers.

In the darkness we groped and grappled with more interest on what was inside a bra than the opening credits of the main feature. Mind you some of them were a bit shabby, the cinemas that is. In fact we often scratched our way home after a session in the old Electric in Barking, the Astoria in Seven Kings and another bug hutch in Manor Park whose name escapes me.

But most of them were wonderful buildings – with soft carpeting, padded seats and internal decorations - the result of thirties art nouveau architecture. In them, between groping and snogging, we'd almost watch the 'big' picture, a cheap 'B' film, a newsreel with 'up-to-the-month' news items, the odd Tom and Jerry cartoon and the old Pearl and Dean advertising film. All that, along with the trailer for the following week's action-packed thriller, passionate love story or 'music and dance' spectacular, for less than a half a quid.

Today's young men have different options when dating a girl for the first time – restaurants or night clubs (which were posh places for rich people wearing dinner jackets in our day). For us it was just 'the flicks', the milk bar or the Saturday Night Hop, though all had their advantages in seduction opportunities.

I had intimate (a word I use advisedly here) knowledge of most of our local picture-houses, but the one that holds the best memory was the old, long gone, Mayfair in Becontree Heath. The Glenn Miller Story had come out many years before, in the early fifties, but films were often brought back for a second run, years later. Well, they still are.

In the early sixties, shortly after I started courting 'Dearly Beloved', after finding her in a glue factory in Manor Park, the Mayfair started a week's showing of that great picture starring James Stewart. I offered her the opportunity of coming with me to see it and of course she jumped at the chance.

Thus it was that on that Saturday night I bought a couple of tickets at the box office, acquired the obligatory box of Black Magic, and we were ushered into the darkness. The programme had already started but had only got as far as the B film so despite arriving late we hadn't missed Glenn. But being late meant that all the back row seats had filled up, so we had to be content with a couple of seats just in front of that row.

That wasn't too bad because we knew the back row seats would be full of courting couples like us anyway, too busy to complain about anyone else. So we sat down, made ourselves comfortable and settled down to an evening of seduction, to Miller music like 'In the mood' and 'Moonlight serenade'.

There we were, happily snogging between mouthfuls of Black Magic and lungfuls of Senior Service, totally oblivious to all that was going on around us and most of the time with my hands well and truly inside her blouse. I have always enjoyed that film and the surroundings and swish decor of the old Mayfair along with the seduction really made it a night to remember.

When we finally surfaced, preparing to join the mad rush to get out before the national anthem and with her doing some buttons up, I happened to glance back at the seats behind us. There was my mum and dad – him smirking, her with disapproval written all over her face.

They'd been sitting there when we'd been shown into the seats directly in front of them, but hadn't felt it necessary to warn me.

60

Definitely not Swan Lake

I saw a news item recently that revealed that, after all these years 'they' are about to close the Ilford swimming baths. The old memory banks immediately switched into gear with visions of post-war urchins, cozzies wrapped in towels under their arms, getting off buses and the whole class being crocodile walked up Highbury Gardens.

I have written before about those early 'splash ins' and our first swimming lessons on the parquet floor of Stevens Road School hall. When it was decided we had learned how to breast stroke through fresh air while standing like storks on one leg risking foot splinters, we were introduced to real water.

I can still hear the echoing whistles and shouts of teachers, taste the rawness of chlorine in my mouth and stinging my eyes, as we clutched our cork boards with one hand. With the other we held up our knitted, and very soggy, woollen cozzies while kicking out to try and make some sort of movement through the water.

It was at another school, the South East Tech in Longbridge Road which had its own pool, that I actually learned to swim – quite well actually. Just as well really, because I was to spend some years in a couple of navies (Royal and Merchant) where the ability to be able to swim was seen to be useful.

But it wasn't just the swimming that brought nonchlorine induced tears to my eyes when I read about Ilford Bath's imminent demise – it was a drier, teenage, activity that did that. On Saturday nights we would flock there (or to the Seven Kings Library, or to Broad Street baths in Dagenham) to hunt for women and for the dancing - and it definitely wasn't your Swan Lake sort of dancing.

As I have pointed out before, today's youngsters ideas about dancing appears to be the skill to wobble and wiggle in front of each other to an incessant beat brought to them by a loudish chap with the modern equivalent of a gramophone record player with huge amplifiers. For us it was the big bands – well locally not always that big – that had us clutching, bopping, hugging and pawing to the Woodchoppers Ball, In the Mood, or Rock Around the Clock. It was girls unlimited, swinging their stiff petticoats around to show off their knickers as they rock and rolled and hoping to be chatted up, bought their drinks in the interval and taken home afterwards.

To Dearly Beloved and me, the old Bill Haley classic, was 'our tune' even though we only met on its second (or was it its third) time around. In those days we could twist and twirl about madly for the entire song before I helped her back to her chair. Now she'd have to help me even get up out of mine.

For me it was those times that cause me to hold the memories of the old baths so dear. Trying not to pick up a bird before half time, in case you had to buy her a drink in the Cauliflower across the road, we would tap our feet, discuss the fanciable ones and 'crash the ash' out of our chromium plated cigarette cases.

A mile or so away in Ilford High Street we had the Palais, but you could always guarantee a 'bit of bovver', there so for the most part we stayed away. Mind you there was occasionally some aggro at the baths too, but it was usually across the road in the 'Cauliflower' and often finished up with someone being 'banned for life'.

Forty-plus years later I was working in the Ilford Recorder offices opposite the baths and went back into the Cauliflower for a lunchtime pint. I got away with it – probably because I had a beard, which I didn't have when they banned me as a teenager.

61

Forget Ferguson, we had Bert Myers

There's an old saying about the spirit being willing but the flesh being weak. What it means is that at my age you think like a teenager, but your body doesn't.

So it is that whenever we see young Ronaldo diving somewhere along the wing, the imagination has us doing it better. If we see Wayne whacking someone's legs with enthusiasm - not with malice of course – we remember our own days in Valence Park burying the studs into someone else's shin pads.

We had our chances, as Venables, Greaves and other 'Valence Veterans' went on to show, but you had to be pretty special even then, and it wasn't easy. For us it was a soggy and heavy leather ball with a lace that made you think twice before heading it. If it was a cloth lace it hurt like hell – if it was a leather one it gave you concussion if you headed it wrong.

For most of us our dreams of playing professional soccer were mostly fantasy – in any case even the likes of the great Stan Matthews was rubbing along on less than twenty quid a week then, so it was hardly a glittering career prospect. We played because we loved it – and we were lucky we had so many parks, pavements and playing fields to do it in.

We also had our local youth club teams – in our case it was Winding Way Athletic – and very willing coaches.

Move over Sir Alec, Mr Curbishly and 'arry' Redknapp – we had Bert Myers.

Ok, so Bert never created any football legends but as with so many others like him in those days, gave a lot of his time to training youngsters like the Mild Bunch and our team-mates. I believe he'd played at amateur level for Ilford AFC, but earned his living as a gas engineer – or at least that's what I was told.

The point is that whatever the weather, Bert would be there for us doing his best to teach us to trap, dribble, shoot and pass the ball intelligently. As his schoolboy players arrived and then moved on to new working careers, Bert would be there for us and he was a hard taskmaster.

Wayne Rooney and the Man Utd lot might be nervous about facing Ferguson's famous 'hairblower' treatment after underperforming, but believe me it was nothing like the 'Bert blasting' we got on training nights if we'd lost the previous Saturday. The man praised us if we'd played a blinder, but told us in no uncertain terms if we'd played a blunder.

In fairness the Winding Way team I played in had a pretty good record when it came to winning and most of us lived in the same street - but there was one side we envied to irritation. The famous Eton Manor club had several boys' teams even then and the one that played in our league never - and I do mean never - ever lost. Season after season they finished up with maximum points, with several of their best players being signed up by professional clubs as they grew up.

But there was one season they didn't quite crack every game and as it happens I was captaining our team that year. We went by bus to their posh ground in East London that day and felt quite 'Alf Tupperish' (the Tough of the Track in the Champion comic), with our rough and ready hand-me-down kit against their superb well laundered shirts and shorts.

It started well because I won the toss and made the right choices about kicking off. Their well-drilled bunch began to pour into our half like smooth silk. However that day they found themselves up against defenders like Buddy Blythe, who idolised that great Tottenham (and Dagenham-born as it happens) full back Alf Ramsey.

That afternoon nothing was going past Buddy and with Ginger Barratt charging in, head down with both feet swirling in the wind, Eton Manor's silky movements began to get a bit ragged. Even when they got past Buddy they came up against our star goalkeeper Andy Meek and that day he seemed to have glue on his gloves because everything stuck to them.

We began to believe in ourselves and held them at bay the first half apart from a few near misses and narrow escapes. Then midway through the second half it happened. I was in my usual slot as right winger but had moved towards the penalty spot when a ball from Eric Johnson out on the left arrived at my feet directly in front of the goal. Their goalie never had a hope, though he took a lot of stick from his pals for showboating. All he had to do was move his feet but he decided to make a very graceful dive to his left – and it went under his body.

It seemed to knock the stuffing out of the 'toffs' and though we never scored any more, they didn't score at all on the day we beat Eton Manor. You know what, after all these years I still love that moment. Thanks Bert!

62

The potato poacher

I've mentioned before how we were urged to 'dig for victory' during that bit of unpleasantness between ourselves and the Fatherland – well at least our mums and dads were, and mine certainly did their bit. I suppose we did ours hunting for the horse manure delivered at the gate by the milkman.

Considering that they came out of East End slums where having a pot plant – usually an aspidistra in the front window - was about as close to gardening as they got, they responded. Admittedly in East Ham mum's house had a backyard big enough to accommodate the lavatory, but she probably never wielded a spade in her life until we moved to the Avenue. Dad having been brought up in the tenements of Wapping certainly never had, but he was a quick learner – well I guess they needed to be in those days.

In the Avenue we had back and front gardens where they created a mini smallholding in which they bred rabbits, chickens and grew every kind of vegetable and fruit they could find space for. If it was edible, they grew it – dad doing the heavy digging work and mum getting hectic with the hoe – mostly in the back garden. Then dad realised that our front garden could do more than grow pampas grass and daffodils and decided to extend his potato crop out there as well.

Ok so it never looked pretty, but it saved them a fortune in King Edwards and meant we had spuds aplenty. At least that was the theory – until someone started nicking them.

Dad would get up in the morning to find one of his 'mounds' had been savaged by what had clearly been an un-neighbourly spade. One or two of the plants had been cast to one side and it was pretty clear that their produce had been plundered. It was sending dad crackers, because the piracy was taking place while the Luftwaffe was visiting us at night. As we waited to be exterminated in our back garden shelter, someone was digging for his personal victory in our front garden potato patch.

I have mentioned before that dad, a bus driver, often finished his shift at night and had to make his way home during the blitz while an air raid was going on. Rather than take shelter in the bus garage he would walk through the ack-ack and bombs whistling down, courtesy of Hermann Goering, because he wanted to be there if we copped it.

So it was one such chaotic night, with the Luftwaffe sending their harbingers of destruction downwards and the ack-ack thumping away all around us in the forlorn hope of hitting something, that dad arrived home out of the blackout. We were all out back in the shelter of course but there, in our front garden and wearing a tin hat (helmet), was a figure industrially digging away by the light of the bomber's moon and the searchlights, in his potato patch.

At first the bloke, who was wearing an ARP armband, did not realise who the new arrival was. Thinking he was just a curious passer by, he even invited dad to join him, saying it was alright because the house was his brother's and he'd told him to help himself.

Well, the guy was certainly no uncle of ours but he had some nerve. As dad, who had been brought up in Wapping which was about a tough a part of the East End as you could get, prepared to point out the error of his ways the potato pincher tried to say he'd picked the wrong house.

'Easy mistake to make in the blackout, mate', he grinned.

Dad never managed to lay a finger on the bloke, he took off so fast - but we did get a result. The geyser went up on his toes so fast he left his 'swag' and as well as our spuds dad found a couple of cabbages and a marrow in the bag as well and we never grew them in the front garden.

Clearly ours wasn't the only field he'd ploughed, and then scattered.

63

Love in the glue factory

I don't believe that, in writing these reminiscences I have ever included how I met Dearly Beloved, and with getting on for fifty years of marriage now under our duvet perhaps its time.

There were three contributory factors – the Baltic, my mother and a Manor Park's desperate need for an engineer. Throw in a few added ingredients, like lust and being the only single bloke in a glue factory full of single young women, and you have lift-off.

I had just paid off what was undoubtedly the worst ship I'd ever been in during four years at sea – (two in the Royal and two in the Merchant navies). I'd joined the extremely mis-named SS Superiority to discover, once we'd reached the frozen swells of the North Sea and then into the Baltic, that she didn't so much sail through heavy seas as slosh off them. I paid off it three weeks later in Glasgow, first chance I got. (A year after I left it, her sister-ship went down with all hands in the Irish Sea).

When I got home my mother, who'd never liked me going to sea in the first place, decided to help find me a job ashore. Well, she insisted actually, and since the merchant navy was going through a bit of a slump at that time with decent ships getting hard to find I agreed, though secretly on a temporary basis, just to pacify her.

I came down the next morning to find she had bought

the local paper and had spent her breakfast going through the job's section for me. One she had underlined was for an assistant maintenance engineer for a firm in Manor Park (that's what I did for a living in those days).

That firm turned out to be a company that had seen better days, manufacturing wallpaper paste and bottling other glues like Gloy. Now it was very much in decline, employing a couple of dozen young girls and a few older blokes but I was offered the job, at about ten quid a week as I recall. Since, in my own mind, it was only going to be a short term proposition, I accepted.

I found myself spending my days walking around the place, usually with an oil can in hand, doing what maintenance engineers do - but I did have several advantages. Most of the workers were local unmarried girls and there was I – a fit young ex-sailor – being dangled in front of them on the top of a stepladder squirting oil into various bits of conveyor belt mechanism. Well, how could they resist?

I was chatted up, given sweets and fags and generally propositioned from 8am to 5pm. Even at lunchtime some of them would often join me on the flat roof to catch some sun with our coke and sandwiches. There were scruffy blondes, pimply brunettes and even a freckled red-head – all anxious to talk to me about the places I'd been to at sea while seducing me. There was me – anxious to talk and optimistic about being seduced.

Then there was Liz – laughing Liz – with her cheerful (despite just having lost her mother) rounded face, surmounted by a great pair of flashing eyes. Her first sight of me had been of my socks. I had been standing on a ladder doing my oiling when I became aware of this girl staring at my feet – well at least at my socks which had a 'B' (for Brian) knitted into them. Her first words to me were not so much romantic as nosey.

'What's the B stand for?'

'Brains', I lied.

'Oh, I thought it might have been for 'brainless' she laughed.

Well, from that moment things went from bad to marriage. Our first date was to see the latest Elvis film (many years later in Tennessee we visited Gracelands) in the West End, followed by a romantic meal in one of the new 'chicken and chip' restaurants. It all led to that fateful day in August 1962 when she lied about 'obeying' me in the same Barking church that other old seaman, Captain Cook, had got spliced.

Oh yeah – I never went back to sea either.

64

Anyone for Denis?

My 'civvy navy' life was partly down to another Dagenham urchin called Denis Tibbett, with whom I drank in Liverpool, Antwerp, New Zealand and sailed through the Panama Canal into the Pacific. We knew each other for less than a year, but for me it was a significant time.

When the Admiralty tossed me back into Civvy Street after a National Service mainly spent driving Motor Torpedo Boats up and down our coast, I went back to the Globe Pneumatic. I'd been a lousy apprentice there before answering my country's call, but works manager George White had to take me back onto the lathes. He didn't want to, but it was the law.

It was full of former apprentices and among them was Denis who'd just come out of the army after doing his two years. For all of us it was very difficult readjusting to civilian life and though I still had ambitions about going back to sea, I couldn't see how. One day, as we 'veterans' shared our tea breaks a 'road to Damascus' suddenly appeared. One of the lads said he'd joined the Merchant Navy as an engineer officer but hadn't liked it so he'd quit.

Talk flowed and both Denis and I were fired up. We took a 'sickie' and a 25 bus to Aldgate where Merchant Navy officers were recruited. We learned that there were three grades of Junior Engineer Officers – 1, 2 and 3. For grade 1 you had to be a university maritime engineering graduate, but 2 and 3 were possibilities if you had done engineering apprenticeships.

In fact Denis had done all of his but although I hadn't, it seemed my Royal Navy service compensated. The irony was that at the end of the day Denis, who was a much better engineer than I was, was graded 3 while I got a 2 because of that naval experience. I also had 'VG-Superior' - a sort of 'mentioned in despatches' - on my record because of something that had happened on the MTBs and that helped as well.

We were told to report for a medical and x-ray that afternoon, so we spent an hour or two in a pub in the Commercial Road while we waited. Our medicals were fine but apparently the fizziness of the Double Diamond also showed up on the x-ray and did cause some concern at first.

Next stop was Leadenhall Street where all the big shipping companies were. We walked into one and were promptly whisked off to see a bloke who offered us both Junior Engineer Officer berths in a ship called the Southern Prince, about to leave for New Zealand. It was all so easy, though surprising Mum with the news later wasn't. She was definitely not a happy mummy about losing her eldest again.

We were sent to join the ship in Hull from where we sailed, first up the Thames to London and then to Antwerp to deliver cargo, before going to pre-Beatles Liverpool to take on cargo for the big trip. This was at a time when the Beatles were probably having their first guitar lessons. All was fine until we sailed from there – straight into a raging storm in the Irish Sea on our way down to the Atlantic.

It was then that my little personal problem resurfaced. Like Nelson's, my stomach never liked the sea either and for over a week I spent my watches going down to the engine room with a bucket in my hand. It was an experience I'd got used to in the MTBs but they were only at sea for hours at a time – this time it was days. My mate on the other hand, the ex-soldier who had never been to sea in his life, was totally unaffected, damn him.

When we got home again Denis decided he preferred Dagenham and swallowed the anchor. I had a few more ships, including a fabulous year in and out of New York in the SS Fort Avalon before time, a shipping slump and matrimony drew a line under my seagoing career.

Ah, well!

65

Hae ye gotta loight, boy?

It gives those of us who have given it up a lot of satisfaction, when asked if we smoke, that we smirk and say that we don't. We feel superior and stronger willed than those who can still only survive on a daily dose of nicotine - well, mixed with a little envy too I guess. Back in the sixties there was a Norfolk postman who had a hit song called 'hae ye got a loight boy', it was all that popular.

The fact is I haven't smoked in over twenty years but it took me over thirty to pack it in. During those three decades I smoked everything but marijuana. I have rolled Old Holborn, coughed up lungfulls of Russian, Colombian and Turkish tobacco, choked on cheap Navy fags, been sick on 'duty free' smuggled Havana cigars and had a variety of pipes clamped between my teeth in efforts to look casual and important.

It all started behind the bike sheds at school. In those days you could buy five Weights or Woodbines, along with a quarter of sherbet lemons, from the corner sweet shop without being questioned. These would be hidden from mum in the handlebars of bikes and lit with red-tipped Swan Vestas matches nicked from the scullery. When really desperate and skint we'd even experiment by rolling up dried apple leaves in Rizla Red papers, but that usually resulted in severe burns as the damn things flared up the nostrils.

The really serious smoking started after our schooldays when we started work. By then we could not only afford to buy big fags like Senior Service and Players in twenties, but cram them into chromium plated cigarette cases. It meant that in places like the Ilford Palais or the Odeon we could literally 'flash the ash' while weighing up the potential talent around us, or sit having a gasper at half time when we were playing football.

That got us started – then for me came the era of cheap fags in the Navy, perhaps the only consolation of being press-ganged into National Service. Every month for only a few bob (shillings) we could buy six-hundred 'Blue Line' fags. Other ex-matelots and rum-rats will know what I mean, and also remember that, in terms of quality, these cigarettes had all the flavour and texture of floor sweepings.

They also had a tendency to spit and fizz, but not half so much as the Russian ones we swapped them for when the Sverdlov brought Kruschev and Bulganin to Portsmouth. Their team played a Royal Navy team and we all went to support our lot, to find the Soviet sailors more interested in swapping their dodgy fags for ours. In tubes only half filled with tobacco, they sparkled and spat with great energy

After the Blue Liners the fags we could get in the merchant navy were different again. By then we could not only afford decent smokes, and 'posh' ones like Benson and Hedges but they were duty free as well. That meant they could be smuggled into various ports as personal smoking property, to be flogged off to local dockies for drinking money.

Some of us in the Southern Prince hid thousands of fags under duckboards in the engine room as we entered Auckland, only to find their Customs never came aboard to search us anyway. That did upset our ship's carpenter who was going to take a few illicit bottles of Scotch into New Zealand but whose courage failed him as we approached the coast and he tossed them over the side. That did not make him very popular with the rest of the crew when they found out.

By the time I was married and breeding, I was trying to pack the smoking up mainly because of the costs involved in raising kids, and was very successful as well. In fact I did it dozens of times over the years - sometimes for hours – but invariably went back to the weed, chain smoking with the chain getting ever longer and more expensive.

I was on sixty a day by the time I stubbed out my last dog-end and they were going up with every budget. I tried everything to stop. Will power was very successful – for about ten minutes – but for a long time the most effective way of packing up smoking was being broke. Trouble was that resulted in a lot of temper-fractured crockery along with major strains on my marriage and my relations with the kids.

In the end it took a handful of chemicals – well a course of pills - determination and the lack of cash combined with a lot of publicity about lung cancer. Now I'm fag-free, nicotine-clean and sneering at those poor weak-willed souls who can't even go out for a pint now because they can't smoke in the pub.

Well, I don't need a loight, boy?

66

The Cameron I'd never vote for

I will not reveal here who I am likely to vote for when Gordon Brown finally plucks up his nerves and lets us go for it, other than to say it's unlikely to be for the BNP or the Monster Raving Looney party.

Politicians all have their good and bad points but I do have a small problem with one of them – a man called Cameron. Not, I hasten to add, that I have anything against the Leader of the Conservative Party who is probably a man very capable of doing his job – it's just his name that gets to me. It has done ever since one of his clan whacked me because he missed his bus one night.

It happened when I was in Rosslyn Road (Barking) school doing the first couple of years of my time in the South East County Tech. Well, it should have been a couple of years but I finished up doing three because as things turned out I was plank of the month so often they could have used me to build a new bike shed.

I suppose I'd never really fitted in. At Stevens Road we had mental arithmetic and sums, not 'maths' and algebra while if anyone had asked where the laboratory was we would have probably pointed them towards the toilet block.

Rosslyn Road's laboratory on the other hand hosted biology and physics classes, the latter lorded over by the aforesaid Mr Cameron. This man never liked me from day one, just because I set fire to my exercise book by leaning it up against a Bunsen burner which happened to be alight at the time.

He liked me even less when I clumsily dropped a couple of his glass bottles, but I suppose the real crunch came around 4pm one Wednesday evening when apparently I beat him onto a 106 bus going home. Not that I knew anything about it until Friday morning, when we had a physics class and his eyes light up as I walked into the lab.

'Ah, Lynch. I've been waiting for you,' he sneered. 'Please come out here to the front,' he added with a clear hint of menace in his voice.

Puzzled, I moved over to stand before him. I could feel my classmates giggling expectantly, while not knowing what was coming any more than I did. At least for them it was a diversion from what was usually a pretty boring lesson anyway.

'What bus do you go home on, boy?' he demanded, knowing full well what one I travelled on because he did as well. He looked up after I'd confirmed it and addressed the court. Yes, I said 'court' because that's what he suddenly turned it into.

'This boy does not know what queues are for. This boy would rather push his way to the front of a bus queue, treading on other people's toes and shoving them out of the way, so he can get to the front,' he told them, adding. 'So let's have a class trial.'

Believe it or not that man made me plead (not guilty, of course), appointed himself prosecutor and judge before volunteering a classmate as my defence counsel. Then he outlined the scene, which naturally I continued to deny and invited my counsel to do his stuff.

He stuttered that perhaps I was in a hurry to get home - I do hope that lad never became a barrister – but the verdict was already in, delivered by unsympathetic classmates more interested in watching the punishment as a spectacle rather than justice.

It was all of that – carried out viciously across the palm of the left hand (though in fairness that was after confirming I was right-handed) with some considerable force in front of a gleeful class.

That day that Cameron brushed aside any protestations of innocence - or talk of an alibi on my behalf and which he wouldn't even check out, which was an injustice. That Wednesday evening I had been doing detention and had missed that bus as well.

67

Don't fly with me...

I was remember watching a TV programme recently about honeymooners in Jersey in the sixties, which is something Dearly Beloved and I did and which left an indelible mark on me. It taught us both a lesson and to this day she mocks that I am an airborne coward.

Look I am no braver, or craven, than the next man. My generation sheltered from the Luftwaffe during the war but at that age we were too young to appreciate anything other than that this was a great adventure and we were not scared.

Then, in later years I sailed through some of the most fearsome seas – including through the Bermuda Triangle and where the Titanic went down – but I was more concerned about the contents of my stomach threatening to reappear, than the fact that we were hanging on for dear life. Yes, fog at sea did cause a bit of concern and the occasional sadistic petty officer usually tried to get his way by fear - but in general we could handle that by keeping out of his way.

Then in 1962, in order to impress my new bride, I promised not only to take her to Jersey for our honeymoon but to fly there. Now, this was an experience I had never really had the opportunity to do. Yes, like the rest of the lads I'd thrilled at the sight of the RAF and Luftwaffe slugging it out over our heads, but peacetime flying was still just for the rich.

By the sixties however, that particular mode of transport was within reach as far as destinations like the Channel Islands and Benidorm were concerned. Anyway she was impressed so, once we'd gone through the essential nuptials, the lad from Dagenham and the lass from Barking (via Manor Park) turned up at Gatwick, full of excitement.

Coolly I escorted her to the airport bar where we had a pint or three and I assured my slightly trembling nervous new wife that she'd be fine once we were in the air. She wasn't wholly convinced and by the time our flight was called she was clearly very much on edge. On the other hand I was a very concerned and attentive young bridegroom reassuringly holding her hand as we boarded the plane and prepared to take off.

Slowly the plane began to move forward onto the runway and I could feel her hand tighten on mine as we picked up speed. Then, suddenly we were in the air and, whoosh, my bottle went completely.

I found myself gasping in terror as the plane soared upwards. Now it was me gripping her hand, and doing it so tightly she was complaining about the pain. I never noticed or heard her moaning. I was too busy looking out of the window where I could see the wings actually shaking and what I imagined were sparks coming out of the engine. The whole plane was shaking and throbbing with the noise, adding to my personal terror, as she managed to free her hand and began to rub the circulation back into it.

That flight only lasted about fifty-five minutes and for me it was an hour I will never forget – and even worse as we got off I knew we had to fly back the following week. The new Mrs Lynch, on the other hand, was thoroughly relaxed and had really enjoyed the experience, excitedly pointing out the Channel Islands as we approached them. It is something she never allows me to forget – not the flight but my performance.

Since those days I have flown a few times, mainly to America and have never got over those fears. I have to steel myself with a few large Scotches to even get onto an aeroplane and once we have taken off I take full advantage of the alcoholic hospitality available. I just do not like it up there!

It is something she loves though, well two things really. She really does like to fly but more importantly she loves to tell all our friends and family about how I change into a craven quivering and terrified wretch inside a moving aeroplane.

68

Hearts of oak are our ships

Our generation invented Elvis, hailed Haley (Bill) - and dashed out of the cinema at the end of a film before they played the National Anthem. We foot-tapped our way through the Saturday Night Hops as we eyed up the available talent, spoke knowledgably of 'Louis' and 'Glenn' and did our best to croon like Crosby and sing like Sinatra (or should that be sin).

Posh music, like the Barking Quintet tried to enlighten us with at school, was not for us and the first notes of Mozart or Beethoven would send us rushing for the door. You see, we'd been brought up with street music.

The Avenue was (still is) a dual carriageway separated by long islands of bushes and trees (now grass), but at the junctions with other roads there was space – useful on VE day for the bonfires and at weekends for the serenades and music of the Salvation Army.

Nothing much happened on Sunday mornings, well apart from the paper shop being open for a few hours and after the UD had delivered the daily cow-juice. The pubs and off licences didn't open until midday, and nobody had money so there were no cars to clean. So, most adults settled for a lie in with the wife, the News of the World and a fag or three. Then the Sally Army appeared and broke the gentle silence with their tambourines, concertinas, breezy hymns and hallelujah choruses.

It was the Sally Ann, so no-one actually shouted abuse from their bedrooms but there was a lot of window-closing and groaning about them inside. Then, once they had rattled their last tambourine and moved off to streets anew, the Boys Brigade marched into our eardrums.

Bugles glistening, drums a-banging and led by a lad wielding a mace which he threw into their air to show off, they paraded noisily through the Avenue on their way to church. They played tunes of Glory too but, unlike the gentle Sally's, theirs was stirring, and very loud, marching music. Our parents had told us how, before the war, they used to tease German marching bands by eating slices of lemon or orange that was supposed to cause the trumpeters to salivate and silence them. That never worked with the BB and to be honest I doubt whether it worked with the German musicians either.

So we kids contented ourselves with prancing along behind them, with a style of marching more in tune with Morris Dancing than what the BB intended. I think their intention was a bit of a Pied Piper tactic to attract a following, but as soon as they halted at the church – we did a runner for Valence Park and its football pitches.

But there came a time when we had little choice but to fall in with the marching bands. A little older, and by then in uniforms kindly donated by the Admiralty in my case, we fell in and paraded to what we described cynically as 'signing on' music, every Sunday morning for Divisions – which is what the Navy called church parade.

Now loyally I claim to this day that nothing can compare with the music of Her Majesty's Royal Marines. No one beat out Hearts of Oak like a bootneck band, but you try keeping in step and arms swinging with a head still throbbing from the previous night's run ashore. The music stirs the blood alright, but the flesh was usually soggy with rough scrumpy (cider).

Today, with no church service to dodge (by claiming to be Jewish or Catholic) after parade, I still have feelings for that patriotic music. Mozart still does little for me though I admit to a fondness for Grieg, Holz and Pavarotti. I proudly thrill now to Jerusalem and Rule Britannia as I watch the Last Night of the Proms, and to this day I still have a soft spot for 'signing on' music.

It's a soggy patch down the end of my garden.

69

A follower of fashion

It made Liz laugh when she saw me wearing it because, apart from sun hats or a panama during our occasional summers, she's never actually seen me in a serious hat. In any case they were protective headgear, not fashion statements. Most of my 'titfer' days took place long before we met so, when I decided to protect my thinning hair with a cap of tweed, she thought it was funny. Personally I think it looks very fetching along with my walking stick and fleece jacket.

The fact was that in those early days most men wore hats – flat caps or trilbys, which incidentally they always lifted in respect when meeting a lady or seeing a passing funeral. We kids certainly did, in fact we wore balaclavas before they became fashionable with the light-fingered blaggers and also covered our unruly mops with those skull-fitting peaked caps that you only see Henley regatta officials wearing these days.

In my urchin days, apart from the balaclavas, I wore caps as a cub, a bush-hat as a scout, berets as a Red Cross cadet, an HMS cap because the Admiralty insisted and a converted busman's cap as an engineer officer in the merchant navy. That does not include the hats and other clobber we wore as post-war teenagers.

I suppose the first sign of approaching puberty would have been the appearance, made more obvious by the

deliberate show of ankles when we sat down and ostenta-
tiously pulled up our trouser legs, of yellow socks. Mothers
hated them of course, because they showed the dirt and
had to be washed more frequently than the ordinary
woollen ones we'd grown up with.

Those ones were often home made - I remember my
gran sitting by our fireside knitting the war away with steel
needles clacking away turning out socks for dad, my
brother and me. They were also darned to destruction when
they were unravelled and the wool recycled for more socks.

The yellow socks were a revelation – our first fashion
statement really – arriving on the market round about the
same time as the light orangy-brown crepe soled 'brothel
creepers' the schools used to ban.

Of course we were fifteen and working by then so we
did have some control over our wardrobe. Had it been left
to mum we would never have been allowed to flaunt our
shiny silken 'kipper' ties. These very wide (about three or
four inches across at their broadest) came in many brilliant
colours and invariably featured a naked, or near naked,
lady standing beneath a palm tree in some exotic location.

We were wearing 'drape jackets' with padded shoulders
and grey flannels, while some went into 'teddy boy' suits
with 'winkle picker' shoes that played havoc with the toes.
I wonder how many potentially great football careers were
blighted by that particular teenage fashion, but it wouldn't
be long before those poor cramped and sometimes
disjointed digits were thrust into heavy boots by the military
for a couple of years.

Just before that happened to me another teenage fashion
began dominating the windows of Burtons, John Colliers
and the other gent's outfitters. In various colours of
corduroy and with a sharp peak, they were the 1950s
versions of dad's old working class flat caps and yes I

couldn't wait to get one. Mine was blue and cost me over a quid as I recall but I only wore it once.

The week after I bought it, and flaunted it 'up West' one Saturday night with the lads, I got the carefully worded invitation from the Admiralty and they had their own ideas on what the well-dressed teenager should be wearing at the time.

I think my brother nicked it once I'd gone, because I never saw it again.

70

Where's ya bin

For us kids, the blitz was a bit of an adventure - part of our everyday life and in which we never really appreciated that the sods flying over us each night were actually trying to kill us. I often wondered what the Wehrmacht would have done if they'd turned up to find thousands of small boys goose-stepping around the country with fingers under their noses representing Hitler's tash. They wouldn't have been happy I guess.

What I do remember very clearly is the great sense of community spirit that kept everyone in the neighbourhood together and involved with each other. Every morning following a night in the shelter neighbours would check with each other that they were alright, and it was genuine concern.

The men - or those that were left behind after the others were called up - did their usual day jobs and then spent their nights fire-watching, or roaming the streets looking for lights in windows, (so they could shout 'put that light out!'). Very often they also spent their weekends drilling with broomsticks on a parade ground with one of the Home Guard platoons.

Our dad was one such man. A London trolleybus driver, in what was called a 'reserved occupation' because of the need to ensure public transport kept operating during the war, he also did his fire-watching stint - looking out for the incendiary bombs Jerry was prone to drop as a bit of a side-show - and in the Home Guard, which became known in later years on TV as Dads Army.

That highly successful show portrayed the Home Guard as a bit of a joke of course, but in reality some of those guys really would have tied knives to broomsticks and had a go if it had become necessary. Captain Mainwaring and his team may have been comic creations, but they also genuinely reflected a serious determination.

So, although it may not have been in a battle zone like in Libya, France or Burma, driving a London bus through darkened streets lit only by the reflective glare of the searchlights and blazing buildings, was no joke. The crews were never even sure how or if they were going to get home (or indeed what they might find when they did).

Fire-watching, especially during the Blitz, was very important even in suburbia. There it was bit like today's Neighbourhood Watch, with the people in the street looking out for each other just as they do today in the fight against crime. Now it's burglars - then it was Adolf's Arsonists and local looters. These little incendiary bombs (I think they were made from phosphorous) could cause quite a blaze if they happened to fall on a house, factory roof or on a fractured gas main.

Our house in the Avenue had a porch which we shared with next door and, because of Dad's fire-watching activities it was also where the local stirrup pump was kept. This pump was little more than a big brass bicycle pump with a rubber hose attached. You dipped it into a bucket, pumped like mad and a stream or spray of water a couple of feet long at best came out of the rubber hose.

Very light and portable, they were never likely to put out a small bonfire, let alone a blazing house but they were sufficient to deal with the incendiary bombs Jerry was happy to lob into our streets in the hope of getting lucky.

For any fires any bigger than that they were a joke. I remember one night raid when Mum was alone in the house with Roy and me (and Gran, her mum) and had no time to get us down the garden into the shelter before the bombs started coming down. We were in the front room and she shoved us both under the table which, while a fairly solid oak job, would not have taken much to become splinters.

Very soon during that raid something was clearly happening outside our house - someone shouted through the letter box to Mum to go and turn her gas off at the main. While she was out in the scullery doing that, I broke the rules and peeked out through the blacked-out window. A huge sheet of flame was roaring up into the sky from the street just outside our front gate. Jerry had apparently hit a gas main with one of his incendiaries and had lit the blue touch paper.

I don't remember how long it took them to get that blaze under control, but I do know that, although the whole house had shaken with the explosion (of the gas, not the incendiary bomb) outside, not one of our windows had got so much as a crack in it as a result.

Certainly the stirrup pump in the porch would not have done much to save us if the hit had been any closer - but nevertheless I did get a good hiding from the old man over it. Well, it was always doing nothing except sitting in the porch all day and whenever we kids got bored we would ambush passing pedestrians with it.

We had a privet hedge outside our house, just high enough for us to crouch down behind with a bucket of water and the stirrup pump. We also had the bushes that ran down the centre of our dual carriageway road and which were our 'jungle' whenever we needed one. So, as people passed by we would leap up either from behind the privet hedge, or from the bushes across the road, and let them have the full pump-load.

It was great fun until Lusher - Police Constable Lusher the bane of our young lives - spotted us while he was working in his own garden four doors away. Despite not being in uniform he charged over and warned us off in no uncertain terms. Do you know, we really grew to hate that man.

In fact by that time the pump was getting very hard to operate anyway, mainly because we were not too fussy where we got the water from. Clearly we could not use Mum's scullery without giving the game away - but the bushes just across the road held many deep and muddy puddles which were very useful for scooping up bucket refills. In fact we even sometimes used the puddles themselves, without benefit of bucket, to ambush our victims.

Anyway, a few nights after Lusher put a stop to our stirrup-pump bushwhacking, we had the little incident involving our gas main, and when Dad's fire-watching pals tried to use the pump while they waited for the fire brigade to come, and no matter how hard they pumped they got barely a trickle out of it.

It turned out that the pipe and much of the brass barrel was full of mud. Lusher blew the whistle on us and I got a bloody good hiding, and a fatherly lecture on sabotaging the war effort. That, on reflection, was a bit strong coming from him, in view of what happened with the pig bin.

These were times of course when 'Dig for Victory' was the great watchword and people like those of us living on the great Becontree estate were all turning their gardens into mini smallholdings. Most of these new gardeners had come out of the East End slums where tiny backyards and window-boxes never really provided a lot of space for rows of spuds, cabbages and runner beans, let alone tomatoes and cucumbers.

So, come the war, they were all learning about gardening as they went along. All the newspapers carried gardening columns, usually featuring a cartoon character of an old grizzled chap with a pipe and big hat, explaining the mysteries of planting, hoeing and harvesting. One of those mysteries centred on the compost heap which of course not only provided good fertilizer, but recycled old dinner leavings as well.

Every self-respecting new gardener had his, or her, own pile of rotting veg down the end of the garden, adding an extra whiff to the excitement of life in the Andersen Shelter, usually planted within smelling distance. These were the 'waste not - want not' years when kids were forced to eat their greens while being reminded that other children in some other countries would have loved to have what we were wanting Mum to throw away.

Recognising that not everyone was into composting, the government had also arranged for galvanised dustbins to be placed at convenient sites in every street, into which the leftover meal scraps could be scraped off the plates, usually by us kids. Then once a week, the somewhat smelly bins would be emptied into equally smelly trucks and sent off somewhere to be processed into pig-swill, for the nation's future bacon to get fat on.

Now as I said, Dad was driving buses throughout the blitz - not ordinary buses but trolley-buses whose overhead power lines were particularly vulnerable to enemy action and would often leave their crews and passengers stranded in all kinds of strange places. It meant that very often he had to walk home to Dagenham from places as far away as Ilford or even Stratford if he had missed the last bus (or in fact had been driving it himself). Clearly very keen to get home to make sure we were alright, he often had to walk and bomb-dodge through the raids.

One night not long after our gas main hit, we were having another particularly heavy raid. This time Mum had got Roy and me into the shelter along with Granny Lacey, but clearly she was also very worried about Dad's safety as well. Hardly anyone had phones then of course, and it was just a case of sitting down there in the shelter, listening to the bombs and guns going off all around us, not knowing where Dad was and just praying he was alright - just as he was anxious about us.

He made it back to the Avenue at the height of the raid that night and was just about to dash indoors when he realised the street was empty and very dark. By the light of the moon, and the searchlights of course, he spotted our local pig-bin sitting lonely and seductively in its usual place, about thirty yards from our door. He realised he had the opportunity of a lifetime - one which would give great impetus to his compost heap and perhaps do wonders for our garden crops.

Still wearing his busman's uniform he dashed over to the bin and picked it up - by its weight he could tell it was over half full – so he went up on his toes in the direction of our house. All this time the war was going on above us, but he opened our door, raced down the passage and through the scullery out into the garden. Mum heard, rather than saw, him come dashing up to, and past, the shelter to his compost heap. There, by the light of the stars he emptied the entire contents of the pig-bin onto it.

Then, shouting to Mum that he was fine and would be back in a minute, he rushed back down the garden and back into the scullery with the pig-bin clutched in his arms. He was half way down the passage when the land mine dropped cross the road.

Now these land mines, which floated down on

parachutes, were very powerful bombs indeed - in fact this particular one completely took out four or five houses on a corner almost opposite us. When it exploded it unleashed a tremendous blast capable of taking doors and windows, not to mention roof tiles, out throughout a wide area. Dad was about half way down our passage with the bin in his arms, when the blast hit our still half open front door, ripped it from its hinges and sent it hurtling down the passageway straight at him.

Before he knew what was happening he was being blown back down the passage, still clasping the bin in front of him (a fact which probably saved his life) and with his own front door joining in the fun and games. He finished up on his back beneath both bin and front door.

By then the ARP and fire-watchers - neighbours all - were out and about and had seen our door go in. Some of them dashed in to see if they could help (or more probably nick something). They found Dad, dazed and disorientated in a heap on the floor with what was very clearly the street's galvanised pig-bin, and our front door, lying on top of him.

This could have been awkward, especially since the bin was sandwiched between Dad and the door; but the old man and his Wapping wit, was up to it. Even as they helped him to his feet, he was thinking fast.

'Look at that', he gasped, 'That bloody pig bin took my door off!'.

No one ever asked about why the bin was empty or why it was between him and the door rather than on top.

71

Blitzed

I hadn't really thought about it for over sixty years, apart from when I'm writing these memories, but a chance remark by a grand-daughter got me thinking.

'What was it like being bombed, granddad?' It turned out she was doing some research for a school project but it did get me thinking – about dark and noisy nights, hectic dashes down a garden path lit by distant flames and shrouded torches.

I've written before about my admiration for the elder generation, the parents of our day, who never showed panic despite being in the front line under the attentions of the Luftwaffe but not so much about us kids.

In fact the blitz lasted a comparatively short while but we kids had already been thrilled watching the Battle of Britain taking place above our heads. We'd gaped open-mouthed at the Spitfires and Hurricanes flying up from nearby aerodromes like Hornchurch and Fairlop to do battle and fantasised about being in one of the cockpits, but that was daylight war. The blitz was something very different and was in the dark.

This was going to bed half dressed, ready to be dragged out for the shelter dash as soon as the siren sounded. It was nights pretending to sleep, wrapped in a blanket on the shelter's crude bunks with only a cheap Woolworth's oil lamp providing a meagre light, listening to the thump of the ack-ack guns around us, the long and monotonous low drone of Goering's bombers and the frightening whine of their cargoes hurtling down towards us from their bomb-bays.

In a sense we were lucky because our part of Dagenham was a fair distance from the ribbon of moonlight called the Thames and which guided the Nazis towards the City, East London and the docks - but we still caught a few anyway. There were the occasions when we went to school in the morning to find some of our classmates absent and said prayers for them in the hall. We took a landmine in the avenue just across the road, that blasted four houses into rubble to create our own local playtime bomb-site (see 70).

We saw plenty of rubble. Our periodic visits to Gran and Granddad Lynch in Stepney meant getting off the 25bus and walking or stumbling through acres of wrecked streets where only a handful of slums, windows already boarded up, still existed. You could see their flat in the distance across an ocean of debris. That vision of the East End never leaves me, especially when anyone condemns the RAF for Dresden.

But back in Dagenham even apart from the bombing we had our moments. After each night's fun and games we'd scour the gardens for shrapnel, so we could give each other some painful 'Chinese haircuts', and spent bullet casings. In the occasional daylight raids we would be rushed into the school brick-built shelter where teachers would lead us in community singing. Believe me singing Oranges and Lemons to a backdrop of the symphony of the ack-ack trying its luck, was an experience in itself.

In later years, in 1973, I almost got blown up by the IRA who left a car bomb outside the Old Bailey on my way to work in the London office of the Birmingham Post. They parked a vehicle full of explosives that I'd passed a few moments earlier on my way to a Fleet Street pub that blew up quite spectacularly – but any shrapnel from that was picked up by the rozzers for forensics.

In any case by then I was in the Bell which was packed with reporters. The pub, which had been there since Christopher Wren built St Pauls, shook with the force of the explosion. This was yards from all the big papers – not one of the 'journos' moved, other than to pick up their booze and go outside with it to view the smoke while they drank it. Well, we all did.

72

I am a 'Vet'

This week, fifty-two years after I handed in my hammock, packed my kitbag and slunk out of Chatham Barracks for the last time, I got recognition that I had done my bit. Not a medal, but a smart gold and enamelled 'badge' and a letter that thanked me for doing my National Service and declared me to be 'a veteran'.

All you need do is send them your name, address and that unforgettable number which is inscribed for ever across every heart that wore a uniform. That brings the badge, in a smart little box, with a note saying it came with the compliments of the Under Secretary of State for Defence and Minister for Veterans. (Call 0800 169 2277 if you're interested).

Now I have written about that part of my life before emphasising that if you ever meet a 'veteran' who said he enjoyed doing his couple of years, you met either a liar or a nut case. But he will also say that it never 'done me no 'arm, mate' – and in that sense he's probably right because in all honesty we did get positives out of it that we never appreciated at the time.

We were separated from our pals and mum's apron strings of course and that was tough. But for almost all of us it was a new world in which our old ones were broadened in a way that most kids today don't experience and in a way that's a shame.

We found ourselves sleeping in big communal huts with Geordies, Scots and Scousers, along with lads from Wales, Devon and Lancashire – in fact from most parts of the UK. We all spoke the same language but in dialects a long way from the cultured accents of the BBC Home Service.

The cuisine they treated us to was usually about as exciting as chewing gum and the tailoring fitted where it touched. We spent our early days in uniform clumping up and down big parade grounds in brand new and very stiff blister-bursting boots with rifles that had probably been salvaged after Dunkirk, carving great ridges in our shoulders.

Oh yes, we were also taught to kill Russians and Communists – well, in my case how to drive Motor Torpedo Boats that could sink Russian ships. We learned to salute everything wearing a peak cap with gold braid that moved and who couldn't be dodged. We were taught the hard way how to clean toilets, scrub floors and even wash our own sheets and underclothes. We also learned how you could walk around the base all day long, holding a piece of paper with no-one questioning you about it.

We learned to make our meagre wage of 28-bob (140p) – even worse in the navy where we were paid fortnightly - last a week. It had to pay for our toothpaste and shaving soap as well as important needs like NAAFI beer, or more likely 'Scrumpy' cider in a local pub because it was half the price of the beer. Weekend leave was fairly frequent but usually meant hitch-hiking or sending an SOS home to Dagenham for the fare or for some pocket money.

It was the same for all of us – whether you wore khaki, air-force blue or the sailor-suits they gave us to swagger around the local dance-halls in – though in our case we did have one advantage with our daily tot of rum. We hated being permanently skint, the shouted discipline, the lousy food and being away from our mates. But without knowing it we were learning a lot about ourselves too.

We learned discipline, how to mix with other lads our age and we learned what loyalty was. A fight in a Portsmouth pub for example, could involve navy, army or air force combatants but anyone involved would always support their own service against the others even without knowing the cause of the problem. We might have hated the bloody navy, but we knew what side we were on in an inter-service punch-up and that never included the use of knives or broken glass beer-mugs, by the way.

It's easy now for people my age to urge governments to bring back some sort of national service, even if only to break up the gangs. Not to learn how to use weapons but to do community work and to instil discipline and self-reliance. As with our generations, it would teach boys how to be men and to be able to act responsibly without the use of drugs or weaponry, rather than feeling sorry for themselves.

I can say that – cos I'm a veteran and I've got the badge to prove it.

73

Jack Frost – the artist

We have had some cold weather this year, no doubt about that, but even so I was surprised to go out to my car one morning to see it's windows covered in a mass of pretty icy swirls and leaf patterns. Haven't seen them in years and never had the heart to spray them away.

Since leaving Dagenham after the wedding Dearly Beloved and I have lived in two houses, a flat, a maisonette, not forgetting the caravan we started out with in Romford. Even though we spent that rather chilly winter of 62/63 in the caravan, I cannot recall ever seeing then or since (until now) the artistic touch of Jack Frost.

Yes it's been cold, knee deep in it at times, over the last forty-five years but I had forgotten what dear old Jack could do to exposed glass and how we had to scrape it off the windows early in the morning. Even after mum had lit the fire downstairs to bring some semblance of warmth into the house at least in one room it still took a while before that, and an icy sun on the window, managed to thaw those delicate patterns out. Unless we scraped them clean ourselves.

Grumbling and shivering in our pyjamas (the only dressing gowns we had were our overcoats and they were on hooks in the passage downstairs), we would keep fingers crossed that the bathroom tap (cold) was running or that mum would come upstairs with a kettle of hot water for the washbowl. Then, rinsed over and dried, we would stumble downstairs seeking to hog the warmth of the fire before being sat down to our morning porridge.

To be honest we were too cold to really appreciate the artistic beauty and delicate designs that blocked the light from coming into that back room. Worse still, when I got paper rounds I had to get up and get out before she'd even got the fire going, so never had a proper chance to warm up anyway. There was a 'wrinkle' often used about stuffing sheets of brown paper up your jumper to keep the chill out. It did actually work to an extent, but you rustled like an open parcel as you swung your arms to keep warm.

No, since those days I have shivered in New York, sailed in the ice packs off Newfoundland and the Baltic, watched groups of Polish squaddies tramping through the snow to mount guard on us as I unfroze the ship's water tank, fallen drunk into snowdrifts in Denmark and walked through blinding snowstorms in Nova Scotia. Never in all those moments, did I feel as cold as we used to when central heating was a rich man's toy.

We were wearing balaclavas long before the bank robbers and 'freedom fighters' discovered them and mittens – gloves with the finger tips missing to give greater freedom of touch – that usually led to frostbitten fingers in snowball fights. We wore boots with studs in them that were slippery at the best of times during the rain and turned into uncontrollable ice-skates at the merest hint of frosty pavement.

Gradually better methods of heating homes, especially after the Clean Air Act, were developed and we all got a little more prosperous – I even had my own proper dressing gown by the time I was sixteen – so our windows were less prone to the etchings of the frost effect.

Well, until last week when I went out to my car of course.

74

Oxford, Essex, West 'am and Stan

Our generation was brought up to be patriotic, stiff upper lipped and, above all, loyal to our country.

The war of course, and melodies like 'There'll always be an England' or with sentiments about 'Hanging out washing on the Siegfried Line' which were designed to make sure we were determined we would never have to learn German, helped all those attributes.

Apart from the mad rush at the end of the cinema programme to get out before the National Anthem was played, the whole nation was on a shoulder to shoulder *'we will fight them on the beaches'* Churchillian footing. I have often wondered what the Wehrmacht would have made of scores of little kids goose-stepping around with their fingers under their noses, mimicking Adolf, if they'd turned up as threatened.

Then there was individual loyalty – which, encouraged by the Hotspur, Wizard and Champion comics, saw its first fights in the playground. Even before we realised that the 'boat race' wasn't just our cockney dad talking about someone's face, we knew it involved some people called Oxford and Cambridge who wore different shades of blue while they were rowing a boat. Once we'd decided which of them we supported that was it for life. To this day I still have a soft spot for Oxford, though God knows why because I can't remember ever having been there.

I mean, most of those of us raking the streets in those days had about as much chance of going to university as flying to the moon, but that never stopped the playground grappling when the subject came up every year. Fists would fly, boots would thud and naked knees would get grazed in the name of one or the other.

We all had to support the Essex cricket team (from a distance) of course, but football was the other big loyalty stimulant. Back in the days when the only foreign names on the first division team sheets were those preceded by Mc/Mac or had surnames like 'O Connor', we all had our favourite teams and our special players who sometimes did not play for our team.

Street soccer between half a dozen ragamuffins always featured names like Arsenal, Charlton or, as in my case, West Ham. There were even occasional punch-ups over who would be what team because even though we were in street urchin kit none of us wanted to pretend we were wearing the colours of rubbish teams you didn't support.

Now this did sometimes cause divided loyalties because very often your soccer idol did not play for your favourite team. In my case that was the legendary Stanley Matthews who, in his heyday only ever played for Stoke and Blackpool – certainly not West Ham. In any case Blackpool was in the first division and the 'Ammers were second division stalwarts, so the two teams were never even likely to meet.

Well, not until January 3rd 1952 when they were drawn against each other in the FA Cup and there was no way I was going to miss that. Complete with my claret and blue scarf and woollen hat I got through the turnstiles onto the 'Chicken Run' early, waiting for my hero to emerge from the tunnel so I could actually see him in the flesh for the first time. Suddenly, there he was – the unmistakeable figure of the wizard of dribble, in person and within a yard or so of me.

I shouted and cheered like everyone and, wonder of wonders, at one point he actually looked over at this cockney kid in claret and blue shouting 'good ole Stan' and he grinned. He grinned at me! My perfect day was complete. Perfect, because we beat them 2-1.

Well, come on – you can only take loyalty so far.

Stan

He grinned at me on the Chicken Run that day
He was the legend who could dazzle
But this was the third round of the FA Cup
And we'd beat his lot to a frazzle.

They called him the 'Wizard of Dribble'
A year later, his day really would come up
In a game that would make Wembley history
And when he'd finally win his Cup.

He'd come down from Blackpool that day
And laughed to hear a Hammers' fan
Wearing the scarf and hat in Claret and Blue
Yet cheering; 'Come on! Good old Stan'.

Till then I had only heard and read of him
Paste his pictures in a book and say
That he was my football hero,
And like him I would always try to play

He was said to be a modest man
Not pushy, arrogant or loud
But on the pitch, he was a genuine star
Well admired, by every sporting crowd

He weaved his patterns down the wing
And with frustrated full backs already beat
Then Stan had no need to rub it in
By turning and going back for a repeat

He came in, bowlegged, from the right
His shoulder dipped, he went out wide
They lunged and had him, only to find
He'd gone past them on the other side

For our country he played with legends
Lawton, Mortenson, Frank Swift and Wright
Wilf Mannion, Finney – they all played better
With Matthews the wizard, out there on the right.

A 'Superstar' – yes he was all of that
But there was much more to Stanley's fame
He had real magic in his boots, and flair
But no ref ever had to take his name

A true gentleman both on the pitch and off
The man had never learned how to foul
They'd try to stop him in any way they could
But retaliate? This man wouldn't even growl.

Yes, he grinned at me that day on the Chicken Run
For us both it was a vital game
The 'Irons' was my team, but he was my God
I cheered when we beat them, just the same

(January 3rd 1952 West Ham 2, Blackpool 1)

75

Squelching down Rosslyn Rd

The sudden outbreak of Siberia we suffered in February (2009), when once again winter caught local councils by surprise, reminded me of so many previous ones, like the big freeze of 1962/3 when my new wife and I lived in a caravan. Then we had the Easter snowstorm a few years later which heralded the arrival of Debbie, our second Lynchling, and I have still not forgotten the day some of us squelched back to school in Barking.

We had a few dodgy winters back in the late forties and early fifties and one of them arrived at a time when I was masquerading as a scholar in Rosslyn Road School. Close to Barking Park, we would occasionally spend our lunchtimes, winter and summer, there usually in and around the boating lake.

During a particularly chilly winter one year, that lake froze over solid and we needed no further invitation. Once someone had chanced their luck and ventured out on it without going through it we were all slipping and sliding across the ice – Torville and Dean in blakeys before they were even born.

Yes we were warned. Miss Coleman, our headmistress, made a special point of forbidding us to go anywhere near that lake while it was frozen over. That, of course, virtually guaranteed that the entire male content of 2E3 would be heading that way as soon as we'd swallowed, or binned, our school dinners.

There must have been dozens of us on the ice that first lunchtime but fortunately the ice was pretty thick close to the bank and it coped with our combined weight. For the half an hour or so we had before the bell went back at the school we skidded and skated to our heart's content. It was a great lunchtime session and in the afternoon we all bragged about it to those who had not come. The next day they did.

That lunchtime there must have been three times the number of boys (the girls were too chicken) on the ice than the day before. Courageously we began to venture further and further out towards the centre, and the thinner ice. Of course the inevitable happened - the ice gave way under about a dozen kids, plunging us waist deep into freezing coldwater.

With the help of those kids still on the solid ice we all managed to clamber back onto it with about ten minutes to go before the bell went for the afternoon lessons. So it came to pass that ten or twelve of us had to squelch back along Rosslyn Road, soaked from the waist downwards and shivering like jellies. Back at school we were not well received by the powers-that-be.

But before she could give us a dressing down, promising us a whack with the slipper as a bonus, for disobeying her command, Miss Coleman was practical enough to see that we needed to undress first. She ordered all the wet ones into the dinner hall, where the radiators were going full blast and it was still fairly warm. We then had to suffer the indignity of having to dry and cover ourselves in hastily provided towels while our sodden clobber was draped over the radiators to dry out.

We were hidden from the rest of the school because the food hall was on an upper floor; but not from the dinner-ladies who had an unexpected display of half naked wet boys to giggle over as they cleaned up after lunch.

In fairness the radiators did their job and by the afternoon break we were wearing our, albeit still damp, clothes as we waited outside Miss Coleman's office for retribution. Along with the whack that came in the form of a few delayed detentions – delayed because of the obvious need to make sure we went home on time to dry out properly that day – and a clump round the ear from mum after reading the letter La Coleman made us carry home explaining the reason for the detentions.

Epilogue

Always remember your roots

There was so much more to our youth
Than Hitler, his Luftwaffe and war
Although of course, to tell the truth
That was always going to be at the core

He'd tried to kill us, as I've already told
In wartime that's not so strange.
But after that we grew up in a different world
One of great social change.

Our parents had known real grinding poverty
In the slums and grime of the East End
Barefoot, scruffy, unwashed and dirty
With only pawnbroker's money to spend.

They'd sworn their own kids wouldn't suffer
The awful kind of upbringing they'd had
Their world could not have been any tougher
Near starvation and in rags poorly clad

So, with the war finally over we thrived
Urchins yes, but kids roaming free
The days our parents craved had arrived
It was why they'd all voted for Attlee.

Vagabonds and rascals, but the Welfare State
Gave us free milk and dinners at school
At last our parents could all celebrate
That their kids could enjoy life to the full.

We raked the streets, played park soccer with passion
All of us with some really great mates
And, even though much of it was still on ration,
We had plenty of food on our plates.

In our teens thick crepe soles and bright yellow socks
Were seen as the height of young fashion.
On Saturday nights, we were quick out of the blocks
Seeking booze, birds and some doorstep passion

We kids had grown up in a very different time
Though it still wasn't all milk and honey
We had no telly or computers, but no grime.
And we had futures that even looked sunny.

Now, just like our parents in their 'good old days'
We want our own kids to do even better
To succeed in life, and their children to raise
Honouring roots that began in the gutter

Brian Lynch

Lightning Source UK Ltd.
Milton Keynes UK
08 February 2010

149762UK00001B/222/P